# power
# spicing

Clarkson Potter/Publishers
NEW YORK

60 Simple Recipes for
Antioxidant-Fueled Meals
and a Healthy Body

# power
# spicing

RACHEL BELLER, MS, RDN

To my parents,
the loving forces of my life;

my four kids, Alexia, Jonah, Evan, and Keira,
for being amazing and making me laugh daily;

and my husband, Mark,
who is my best friend

# Contents

# Introduction

Spices have never been hotter—and I'm not talking about that burning sensation you get from crushed red pepper flakes. People everywhere are spicing up their dishes, drinks, and even desserts, not only to add flavor but to boost their nutritional values. Suddenly exotic spices like turmeric, which used to get little attention outside of Indian cuisine, are appearing in American breakfasts.

And I say bring 'em on! As a Registered Dietitian Nutritionist, I can tell you that the most effective eating plans are those that taste great. Spices transform healthy dishes from bland to in demand—a simple bean salad can take on a rainbow of personalities depending on the spices used. But there's so much more.

Spices pack amazing medicinal properties. Our ancestors developed spicy remedies for all sorts of ailments. And today we're still discovering new benefits. As I've learned through my years of research, spices add "daily power" to our lives by promoting health and decreasing the risk of illnesses such as heart disease and cancer. Spices and herbs are the easiest, tastiest, and most affordable way to boost your health every day.

In 2013, an article from the American Institute for Cancer Research discussed how just a pinch of any spice could deliver antioxidant, anti-inflammatory, and cancer-fighting benefits. In just the past five years, more than 1,900 studies have been conducted on turmeric; 1,600 on cayenne; 1,400 on garlic; 800 on clove; 750 on cinnamon . . . and the list goes on! These studies reveal that the spices we take for granted are really super-concentrated sources of phytonutrients (a.k.a. natural plant compounds) with a wealth of health benefits. For instance, did you know that cloves have the highest antioxidant concentration of all foods? Here's another one: While you know that broccoli is good for you, I bet you didn't know that flavoring it with garlic powder can boost the meal's anticancer properties, and sprinkling on some cumin and cayenne may help your body burn fat.

Then there's my favorite discovery, which I call "spice synergy." When used together, certain spices boost each other's powerful nutritional effects. For example, cacao (the basis of chocolate) helps your body absorb more of the anti-inflammatory nutrients from turmeric, so using these two spices in combination yields the most potent effect.

All this research and experimenting with spice combos inspired me to up my family's spice game. Last year I launched my own brand of spice blends called Rachel Beller's Power Pantry (and no, you don't need to buy them—in this book I'll show you how to make your own combos at home), and I now keep them on my dining table alongside the salt and pepper. I'm thrilled to watch my family of finicky eaters use spices regularly.

Now it's your turn.

This book unlocks the potent power of spices (which come from plant roots, bark, or seeds), herbs (which come from plant leaves), and blends. I've combed through the science for you to reveal the jaw-dropping health benefits, and included shopping tips and easy recipes to make spices part of your daily routine. By the end of this book—or even just a few chapters—I hope you'll start introducing these habits into your daily routine:

## Power up.

I've seen so many friends and patients spend way too much money on the latest and greatest superfood, only to find a half-used package in the back of their pantry a year later. Spicing isn't a trend; it's a great habit to form. With just a pinch, you can dramatically double—or triple!—the nutritional power of your dishes, even after they're cooked. You can and should add spices to everything, whether you're cooking or dining out (that's why I bring spice blends with me to restaurants, and I hope you will, too).

## Go for variety and combos.

Some say variety is the spice of life, and I'll add that a variety of spices makes life even better! While spicing consistently is key, don't hold back: try out my DIY spice combinations on page 51, or experiment on your own.

## Cook more.

To some, packaged foods taste better than homemade. But most manufactured, packaged meals fill you with too much bad stuff and not nearly enough good. The spice-intensive recipes in this book, however, are designed and tested to be nutritious, delicious, and easy. Even my noncooking brother now prepares them on a regular basis! If you include at least two beverages and five meals from this book in your weekly meal rotation, you'll experience a big difference in how you feel—for now and for life.

Above all, I hope *Power Spicing* will forever change the way you think about spices. By adding them to your daily routine, you'll transform your kitchen pantry into a tiny pharmacy and convert your dining room into the world's tastiest health club. So don't hold back: Spice up your dishes (and your health) with just a pinch!

Happy Spicing!

# Power Spicing 101

## Five Reasons to Spice Up Your Life

Why should you get your spice on? Yes, of course, spices taste great, but here is why you should make sure they're part of every meal, even in drinks and desserts.

### 1 You need your daily antioxidant and anti-inflammatory fix.

Antioxidants are compounds that help protect and repair your body's cells. They do so by blocking unstable molecules known as free radicals, which wreak havoc on your body by damaging cells. Antioxidants protect your DNA, preserve your cellular function, and promote your longevity.

Once upon a time everyone thought blueberries were the best source of antioxidants. We now know that spices far outshine produce. A 2010 study by Harvard and the University of Oslo tested the antioxidant levels of over 3,100 foods and made some eye-opening discoveries: A teaspoon of ground cloves has about 50 percent more antioxidant content than a half cup of blueberries! If you add just a few pinches of cinnamon and nutmeg to the mix, you more than double your antioxidant dose. And imagine the flavor!

As for inflammation, it is your body's natural response to injury and illness. You know when you have a cut or bacterial infection, and that part of your body starts to experience swelling, heat, and redness? That's inflammation helping your body heal. But long-term (i.e. chronic) inflammation has been linked to some cancers, rheumatoid arthritis, heart disease, Alzheimer's, and more. Studies have shown that spices can boost genes that promote anti-inflammatory processes and reduce pro-inflammatory ones. And even though some spices may taste hot, they actually "cool down" (reduce inflammation in) your body.

### 2 Spices help fight cancer.

The anti-inflammatory and antioxidant effects of spices may help keep regular cells from transforming into tumors. But spices may also attack a wide range of cancers, including breast, colon, gastric, lung, prostate, skin, and pancreatic. Hundreds of laboratory studies have shown that compounds in spices may inhibit cancer cell growth, block cancer cell proliferation, prevent metastasis, and even kill damaged cells before they reproduce. Other spices may enhance your immune system so that it can annihilate tumor cells, or they may block the formation of blood vessels to tumor sites, cutting off their access to nutrients and fuel. While more studies are necessary to further explore the anticancer properties of spices, enough research has shown that spicing is a promising cancer-protective strategy.

## 3 You might lose weight more easily.

Of course, weight loss mostly depends on eating appropriate amounts of nutritious foods and maintaining an active lifestyle. But spices *do* offer extra help when the going's tough—think of them as "sprinkles of support." For example, the major compound in cayenne pepper is capsaicin, which has been shown to help burn some extra calories while reducing your appetite. A 2014 Iranian study demonstrated that just a half teaspoon of ground cumin may lead to greater weight loss. And spices such as fenugreek, ginger, nutmeg, and orange peel may reduce your hunger and regulate your digestion by activating hormones that make you feel full.

## 4 You'll make your gut happier.

Spices and herbs have antibacterial effects, but throughout most of history, we didn't know how spices affect the all-important bacteria in our guts. Then, a 2017 study published by scientists at UCLA found that extracts of black pepper, cayenne, cinnamon, ginger, oregano, and rosemary promoted the growth of helpful bacteria, such as those found in commercial probiotics. In addition, the spices inhibited growth of nasty microbes often found in unhealthy digestive tracts. Although more research needs to be done, I'm excited about the potential of everyday spices and herbs to regulate the gut microbiome.

## 5 You'll eat more real food.

The best healthy eating plans are those you stick with, and I know that boring diets get dropped in no time. People need flavor, variety, and deliciousness in their meals! If you want to take steamed broccoli from zero to zapper, all it needs is a few pinches of garlic, pepper, and cayenne, plus a squeeze of lemon juice. Dress oatmeal for success by decking it out with cinnamon and orange peel. The possibilities are endless.

I tell my clients to spice things up consistently over time—pinches of goodness add up to greatness!

While some of this may be news to you, people have used spices as medicine for thousands of years. Now scientists are starting to reveal how these spices work to benefit our health. Although many studies are still in the lab, others have already shown that small amounts of spices can make a difference in actually lowering the risk of disease.

I do *not* recommend relying on pills or supplements that consist of isolated compounds from spices, such as curcumin from turmeric or piperine from black pepper, as you'll miss out on additional benefits. Spices contain multiple phytochemicals—for example, turmeric doesn't just contain curcumin; it also has additional compounds such as carotenoids, xanthophylls, and eugenol. If you take an isolated curcumin supplement, you'll miss out on these other nutrients! You'll also miss out on potential synergistic effects that come from spices (see Power Couples, page 38). If you do take supplements on top of power spicing, consider it "extra insurance" and always discuss the idea with your physician.

# Your Must-Have Spice Starter Kit

Ready to build a power pantry in your kitchen? Ideally you should use as many spices as possible. These are all power players in my kitchen, and you can use them in countless dishes. What's more, you can mix many of them together to create your own sweet or savory blends. Stock up and spice up!

- Basil
- Black pepper
- Cardamom
- Cayenne
- Ceylon cinnamon
- Crushed red pepper flakes
- Cumin
- Garlic
- Ginger
- Oregano
- Paprika
- Parsley
- Thyme
- Turmeric

# Tips and Tricks

## Whole vs. Ground

In general, whole spices rule. You know exactly what you're getting (no fillers, no contaminants). They're fresher and more potent, and they last longer on the shelf. Use a small coffee grinder or a mortar and pestle to grind small batches at once. Now, I get it—life is crazy busy and the realist in me knows that 8 out of 10 times we need to reach for the quick and easy solution. I use ground spices most of the time—they have powerful flavors and health benefits as long as you buy good-quality products and replace them frequently.

## Shopping

When buying ground spices, be careful! There are a lot of questionable dealings in the spice market, including instances of dyes added to chili powder and turmeric; papaya seeds subbed in for peppercorns; and sawdust, mold, grass, insect parts, and other unpleasant objects ground into spices. So here are my tips to shop for spices with confidence:

▶ **Avoid cheap grocery store spices, since they tend to be low-quality and sit on shelves for too long!** Chances are you're buying stale spices, as spices oxidize and lose their flavor and health benefits over time.

▶ **Avoid bulk bins.** There usually isn't a brand attached to bulk spices, so you can't know whether the company sourcing them has high standards. In addition, grocers may not replenish the bins frequently, so the spices are often exposed to light and inconsistent temperatures, which can cause deterioration of flavor. Shop at ethnic grocery stores, specialty spice shops, and online.

▶ **Read the label.** Be sure to avoid fillers and additives such as artificial colors and flavors, preservatives, and anticaking agents (such as sodium aluminosilicate, potassium ferrocyanide, calcium carbonate, calcium silicate, and silicon dioxide).

▶ **Choose organic.** Conventional spices are often sterilized by fumigation or irradiation. Organic spices are sterilized via steam treatment or dry heat, both of which are less toxic methods.

## Storage

Spices and dried herbs are sensitive to light, heat, and moisture, so protect them! I recommend airtight glass containers, which will help preserve the spices' essential oils (that's where the flavor and health-boosting qualities come from). And though a colorful display of spices and herbs brightens up a countertop, sunlight can easily oxidize the spices, leaving them dull and flavorless and rendering their antioxidant compounds useless. Instead, store spices in a dark area such as a pantry or cupboard. While storing spices above an oven or stove may be convenient, this exposes them to additional heat and humidity, which can cause clumping and the potential for mold.

Store fresh herbs in the refrigerator and use them quickly, since they usually won't last longer than a week. To keep them fresh, snip off the bases of the stems, remove wilted or discolored leaves, and stick the ends in a glass with an inch of water. Cover the top of the glass with a paper towel and secure it with a rubber band.

## Shelf Life

Spices lose their flavor and potency over time. Whole spices (think cinnamon sticks and peppercorns) and dried herbs typically last one to two years. Ground spices and dried herbs are good for about twelve months—any longer and their flavor and health benefits slowly deteriorate. If you don't remember when you last used a spice in your cabinet, take a sniff. If there's still a potent aroma, you're good to go. If the scent is faint, it's time to replace.

## Cooking with spices

▶ **Add spices during the beginning of cooking and fresh herbs at the end.**

▶ **"Blooming" spices is an important process that helps release the spices' natural oils, evenly distribute the flavors into the dish, and boost the absorption of some beneficial compounds.** To bloom any spice, heat some oil in a small pan over medium-high heat, add your aromatics (such as onion or garlic), then add the spices and let them cook for about 30 seconds, being careful not to let them burn. (You can do this with whole or ground spices— my favorites to bloom are cumin, coriander, turmeric, and fennel.) Then continue with whatever recipe you are using.

▶ **Do not shake spices straight out of the shaker over the pot or pan while you are cooking.** The steam can rise into the shaker or jar, causing the spice inside to cake, clump, and possibly mold. Instead, pour spices into a small spoon or your palm away from the pot, then sprinkle them into the dish.

▶ **Crush dried herbs with the back of a spoon or between your palms before adding.** This releases the herbs' oils, which results in more flavor.

▶ **After mincing or crushing fresh garlic, let it sit for 10 minutes before cooking.** This allows sufficient time for a chemical reaction that forms allicin, the major health-boosting compound.

▶ **Make a few of my DIY spice blends (pages 51 to 53).** This way you can easily add multiple spices to dishes without having to take out four or five jars each time you cook!

*Are you ready to meet the spices?*

# Meet the Spices

Thousands of studies have investigated the potential benefits of spices and herbs. While more research is needed in terms of specific dosing and generalizability of results, my motto is to incorporate a wide range of spices into your cooking for the most benefits possible.

# Allspice

Selectively kill cancer cells while leaving healthy cells alone and prevent cancer cell proliferation

Reduce inflammation throughout the body

Fight diabetes by lowering blood sugars and helping with carbohydrate metabolism

Combat stress by modulating neurotransmitter release and exerting antioxidant activities in the brain

Protect against diarrhea and stress-induced gastrointestinal discomfort (read: less cramping, bloating, and urgent trips to the bathroom)

Prevent stomach ulcers

Soothe indigestion by stimulating digestive enzymes

Have antibacterial and antifungal effects

Alleviate symptoms of menopause due to its hormone-modulating properties

Decrease blood pressure

Before we go all in, let's clear up one popular misconception: allspice is *not* a mix of several different spices. (I'll do all the mixing in this book!) In fact, it is made from pure dried berries of the Caribbean *Pimenta dioica* tree. The British named it "allspice" in the seventeenth century because it seemed to combine four aromas in one: those of cinnamon, black pepper, nutmeg, and cloves. Its key bioactive ingredient is eugenol, which packs in all-around benefits!

.............................................................................................

Allspice lends a rich, complex flavor that can be used in both sweet and savory dishes. Sprinkle it on breakfasts as part of the Sweet Success Morning Power Blend (page 53). You can also drop a few whole allspice berries into a stew or a pot of beans to infuse it with a more complex aroma.

# Basil

So you know fashion "basics"—items that are a wardrobe staple, like a denim jacket or a little black dress? It's time to make basil one of your power pantry basics! From Italy to Indonesia, basil is a timeless, consistently in-demand ingredient, and you'll find it in almost everything from salad dressings to sauces to cocktails.

While you might think of basil as part of the "holy trinity" of Italian cuisine—along with garlic and tomato—it's a multipurpose herb that can top almost any type of dish. Best of all, basil has health perks that are always in style.

The herb that scientists call *Ocimum basilicum* (the species name that includes the sweet, Genovese, and Thai basil varieties) is a rich source of phytochemicals. These antioxidant compounds help to protect your body on a cellular level.

**STUDIES SHOW THAT BASIL MAY:**

Prevent stomach ulcers caused by stress, medications, and alcohol

Promote cardiovascular health by maintaining healthy blood vessels

Reduce blood sugar spikes after a meal by slowing glucose release into the bloodstream

Reduce inflammation and degeneration in brain cells

Fight diarrhea

Have potent anticancer properties—it may protect against DNA damage, kill cancer cells, and prevent tumor cells from spreading.

..........................................................................

There are over 150 varieties of basil, and they all pack health benefits. The key is to buy organic—a 2014 study from the University of Maryland found that organic basil contained greater concentrations of antioxidant, anti-inflammatory, and anticancer components than conventional basil.

Here are two of my favorite ways to use basil:

**Salad dressing:** Add chopped fresh basil to your usual combination of balsamic vinegar and extra-virgin olive oil. For extra credit, top that salad with some slivered almonds, pine nuts, or avocado. Research suggests that the vitamin E in those foods has a synergistic antioxidant effect with the rosmarinic acid in basil.

**Tea time:** Pour hot water over 1 tablespoon dried basil in a mug and steep.

When it comes to spices, black pepper is as common as it gets. It's so ubiquitous that we don't think about it much, but it yields an impressive number of nutritional benefits.

You may have heard that black pepper makes turmeric, another power spice, even more powerful. Studies show that pepper can enhance the effectiveness of curcumin (the anti-cancer nutrient found in turmeric) by up to 2,000 percent.

That extra kick comes from pepper's signature component piperine, which helps make nutrients more "bioavailable" (i.e. easier for the body to absorb).

Pepper may also boost such other nutrients as vitamins A, C, D, E, and B; beta-carotene; selenium; magnesium; calcium; and iron. It can also increase absorption of the antioxidants in fish and meats, red wine, and green tea.

The best part? A little bit of pepper can go a long way. Scientists are finding that it may only take about $\frac{1}{8}$ teaspoon of black pepper to yield these bioavailability-boosting benefits. It's that easy!

........................................................................................

Grinding whole peppercorns yourself will impart a fresher flavor than store-bought ground pepper.

Pepper is already used in nearly every savory dish, so for something new, try sprinkling some in a mug of matcha green tea. It may sound bizarre, but it increases availability of the star antioxidant in green tea. For even more synergistic power, add a squeeze of citrus juice.

# Cacao

All praise . . . chocolate? Or more precisely, the bean that chocolate comes from: cacao.

Pure cacao is *packed* with natural chemicals called polyphenols that convey major antioxidant and anti-inflammatory effects. These polyphenols may also boost your body's natural antioxidant enzymes, which help protect you against cellular damage. In fact, cacao contains twice as many polyphenols as red wine and three times as many polyphenols as green tea. Some studies show that if you combine cacao with wine or tea, you could have a powerful synergistic effect.

You should opt more often for the pure powder instead of a chocolate bar because many chocolate bars contain milk, which may block the absorption of the valuable phytonutrients in cacao. But even among the powders, not all are created equal. Let's take a look:

**Dutch-Process Cocoa.** "Dutched" or "alkalized" cocoa is processed with chemicals and heat, which substantially reduces the antioxidant content—almost a 98 percent loss of epicatechin and an 80 percent loss of catechin (two of the heart-healthy polyphenols found in cacao). Avoid!

**Natural-Process Cocoa.** Cocoa powder is processed at high temperatures, resulting in a loss of nutrient content. Some companies also mix fillers (sugars, sweeteners, and powdered milk, oh my!) into cocoa powder. Also avoid.

**Cacao.** Cacao powder is minimally processed at low temperatures, so it retains a high concentration of enzymes, vitamins, and nutrients. It's the closest you can get to the raw bean, but in powder form. Cacao is my top pick for maximum health benefits.

*I routinely add cacao to smoothies, teas, oatmeal, sweet snacks, and even soups, as in the Black Bean Choco Chili (page 98).*

## STUDIES SHOW THAT CACAO MAY:

Inhibit cancer cell growth and kill already existent cancer cells

Increase tamoxifen's (a treatment for breast cancer) cancer-fighting effects

Improve cardiovascular health by lowering blood pressure, reducing bad cholesterol, boosting good cholesterol, and maintaining the integrity of your blood vessels

Help prevent diabetes by reducing insulin resistance

Sharpen mental function by promoting neuronal growth and blood flow to the brain

Protect against aging and cognitive decline, possibly reducing the risk of Alzheimer's and Parkinson's diseases

Help keep skin smooth by increasing circulation and hydration for the skin, while protecting against ultraviolet-induced damage

Decrease pro-inflammatory chemicals in the body

Soothe moods associated with anxiety and depression—no wonder we turn to chocolate when we want to wind down!

Enhance "tumor-killer" cells and impede development of breast, skin, and colon cancer

Lower your blood pressure and reduce the risk of stroke

Debloat your tummy through diuretic effects

Stimulate your gut, relieving constipation

Help relieve abdominal spasms (as in irritable bowel syndrome)

Protect against stomach ulcers

Soothe asthma symptoms by relaxing the airways in your lungs

Reduce cholesterol and triglyceride levels, protecting your blood vessels from plaque buildup

If you enjoy Indian food, you'll know the distinctive sweet, woody flavor of cardamom. It originated in Sri Lanka and is now grown and embraced around the world—from China to the Middle East to Scandinavia—and yet it has only recently started to become popular in American kitchens. Cardamom has so much to love: a sweet and spicy taste as well as a wealth of health benefits, largely due to its major phytochemicals cineole and limonene.

High-quality cardamom is expensive, but it's so potent that most recipes need only a teaspoon or so. And given its health benefits, it's worth the investment! There are two types of cardamom: green and black. Most recipes, including lattes and desserts, call for the green variety, which is slightly sweet and floral, while black cardamom is more smoky and better suited for savory curries and stews.

I typically use ground cardamom in my dishes because it's quick and easy, but you can also buy whole pods and grind them with a mortar and pestle for ultimate flavor release. I also add whole cardamom pods to ginger tea or black tea to give it a fragrant twist—just smash them with the back of a spoon prior to adding.

# Cayenne

The "cayenne-do spirit" is a phrase that enters my mind whenever I recommend this spice to my clients. That sizzling sensation your taste buds get from cayenne pepper isn't just for fun. It's telling you that you're getting a healthy dose of capsaicin, the compound in cayenne pepper that is responsible for burning fat, among other things.

Cayenne is not just "hot" in the spicy sense. The capsaicin in cayenne literally raises your body's core temperature, causing you to burn some extra calories. These calories may add up over time, and every bit counts when it comes to ongoing weight loss.

You can add a pinch of cayenne to pretty much any dish you want to kick up a notch in the heat department. If you're sensitive to spice, start with ½ teaspoon or so, then work your way up.

- Add some sizzle to your salads by stirring cayenne into your oil-and-vinegar dressing.
- Chase a spicy meal with some antioxidant-rich red wine, berries, pistachios, or chocolate. One study found that capsaicin combined with the antioxidants found in such foods produced more cancer-preventive effects than either compound alone.
- Sprinkle cayenne on cruciferous vegetables (broccoli, cauliflower, Brussels sprouts, cabbage, etc.).
- Capsacin combined with a compound in these vegetables may reduce the migration and invasion of cancer cells. Shake up some apple cider vinegar, lemon juice, and cayenne (page 65) for a drink with plenty of flavor and a slight throat-burning sensation . . . with metabolism-boosting benefits.

## STUDIES SHOW THAT CAYENNE MAY:

Kill tumor cells responsible for various cancers—pancreatic, colon, prostate, liver, esophageal, bladder, skin, and lung—while leaving normal cells unharmed

Stimulate digestion by promoting release of bile acids and digestive enzymes that break down food

Lower cholesterol and triglyceride levels, which promotes heart health

Reduce the risk of stomach ulcers

Exhibit antioxidant properties

Alleviate inflammation and improve symptoms of autoimmune diseases such as rheumatoid arthritis and multiple sclerosis

Decrease blood glucose and increase insulin release, possibly helping to prevent diabetes

Help absorb iron, zinc, calcium, and the antioxidant beta-carotene

# Cinnamon

**STUDIES SHOW THAT CINNAMON MAY:**

Help regulate blood sugars, improve insulin sensitivity, and reduce hemoglobin A1C levels (a marker of diabetes)

Fight breast, lung, and prostate cancers

Reduce chronic inflammation

Prevent heart disease by decreasing total cholesterol, triglycerides, low-density lipoproteins (LDL, or "bad" cholesterol) as well as increasing high-density lipoproteins (HDL, "good" cholesterol)

Lower blood pressure

Decrease the risk of Alzheimer's disease by inhibiting the buildup of harmful proteins in the brain

Reduce the risk of gastric ulcers by stunting the growth of *Helicobacter pylori,* the bacteria that is often implicated in ulcerations leading to stomach cancer

Sure, everyone knows cinnamon—that sweet and spicy, all-natural alternative to sugar. But beware: Most of the cinnamon in grocery stores isn't the type you should indulge in!

Most cinnamon—whether it's labeled cassia cinnamon, Saigon cinnamon, or just "cinnamon"—contains a liver-toxic compound called coumarin, which data suggests may be harmful if you use more than 2 teaspoons per day. Instead, look for the lighter, sweeter variety known as Ceylon cinnamon, which has 1,200 times less coumarin than its counterparts. Ceylon cinnamon is native to Sri Lanka and Southern India.

Check the label on your ground cinnamon; if it doesn't say Ceylon, it's probably cassia. With sticks of cinnamon, the Ceylon variety typically has multiple, thin layers of bark, while cassia has only one thick layer.

# Cilantro

Looking for a strong, fresh flavor? Go with cilantro! (*Cilantro*, by the way, is Spanish for coriander. I'll tell you about coriander seeds on page 22).

Cilantro isn't for everyone. While its strong flavor tastes like citrus to most people, for about 10 percent of the population, cilantro leaves a taste like soap. These people are not being picky—they're genetically inclined to taste cilantro that way.

If cilantro tastes fine to you, do keep in mind that it's great for cleaning your insides. Scientists have used cilantro to filter heavy metals out of drinking water, and some studies have found that cilantro can decrease lead and cadmium buildup. So forget those juice cleanses (which are not based on any scientific proof); if you really want to clean up your inner act, get your cilantro on!

Contain flavonoids and polyphenols that convey powerful antioxidant effects

Exert antitumor activity and inhibit metastasis in breast cancer

Protect the liver from chemical damage

Reduce system-wide inflammation

Decrease blood sugar and cholesterol levels

Protect the skin from ultraviolet (UV) radiation, which can cause wrinkles, roughness, hyperpigmentation, and sagging

...................................................................................................................

You can buy fresh cilantro everywhere. Simply pick a bunch with bright green leaves without any signs of wilting, and either use it right away or briefly store it in your fridge. Fresh cilantro makes a great topper for stews, curry, tacos, and fish dishes. You can also use dried cilantro, which keeps longer and blends well but has a more subtle flavor.

# Cloves

Reduce system-wide inflammation

Kill tumor cells: Cloves possess anti-tumor properties for skin, colon, breast, cervical, and gastric cancers

Lower blood sugars, reducing the risk of diabetes

Help you metabolize and detoxify chemicals and drugs

Promote liver health with targeted anti-inflammatory and antioxidant effects

Preserve bone density and strength

Protect the stomach from ulcers

Kill bad bacteria, including *Escherichia coli*, *Staphylococcus aureus*, and *Bacillus cereus*—all nasty bugs that can make us sick

When most Americans think of cloves, they picture the seasoning on roast turkeys or (the horror) in cigarettes. What they don't think about is the fact that cloves are a true super spice—and one that's readily available and affordable.

Cloves are the flower buds of a towering tree originally from the Maluku Islands near Indonesia. The spice has been traded worldwide for four thousand years, but only now is research revealing why cloves work the way they do.

Cloves have the highest antioxidant concentration of any other food. Yes, even more than chocolate, blueberries, blackberries, and cherries! Cloves even have three to fifteen times the antioxidant value of other spices and herbs. This claim does not mean the others are weak, but cloves are definitely an antioxidant powerhouse!

You can simmer whole cloves in broth or soups to add a warming autumnal flavor, but make sure to strain any whole cloves from your finished dish (the French word for them is related to the word for "nail," and for good reason!). In my opinion, the easiest way to use cloves is ground—they are a great complement to cinnamon and other sweet spices.

# Coriander Seed

**STUDIES SHOW THAT CORIANDER SEED MAY:**

Reduce blood sugars and increase insulin secretion, conveying antidiabetic effects

Lower total cholesterol, triglycerides, and LDL cholesterol, and increase HDL cholesterol

Relieve pain associated with arthritis and other inflammatory diseases

Help debloat due to their diuretic effects

Have an antimicrobial effect against a wide range of bacteria

Lower blood pressure

I've already told you about coriander leaves, which most Americans call cilantro. Time to talk about the seedy side of coriander, which is just as amazing. The seeds are actually dried coriander fruit. When roasted, they have a subtly warm flavor that's nutty, spicy, and citrusy. Of course, I prize them for what they can do for your health—not just your taste buds!

Coriander seeds assist with digestion all along your gastrointestinal tract. They may enhance gastric acid secretion and intestinal enzyme release, thus helping break down food so that nutrients can be optimally absorbed. Coriander seeds may also help shuttle food through your gut and debloat your tummy with their diuretic effects. Yes, we're talking about making you regular and comfy after a big meal!

While you can toast whole coriander seeds for a maximum flavor punch, I've found that the powder is a convenient way to flavor dishes. Coriander is a common component of garam masala, curries, and stews.

# Cumin

Promote weight loss

Have antidiabetic, anticancer, antibacterial, antifungal, and antiviral properties

Protect cellular DNA, proteins, and lipids from damage

Help digest fatty meals and alleviate diarrhea

Lower total cholesterol levels, reducing the risk of heart disease

Enhance memory and reduce stress

I ask all my clients and family members to get clued in on cumin. It practically follows black pepper in terms of global popularity. This savory spice is rich in a wide variety of antioxidants and health-boosting compounds. After you learn what else cumin can do for your health, you'll start using it more, too. Cumin is rich in a wide variety of phenolic acids and flavonoids (antioxidant and health-boosting compounds)—in fact, it has higher antioxidant activity than vitamin C!

Don't confuse cumin with sweet cumin (another name for star anise) or black cumin (a name for Nigella sativa, a totally different plant with smaller and darker seeds). Cumin makes a great salt substitute, since it adds a savory edge to just about anything. I love sprinkling cumin on eggs, roasted veggies, hummus, and nuts.

# Fenugreek

Fenugreek isn't always easy to find in the United States, but it should be! Its aromatic, golden seeds are used to make Indian and North African dishes, particularly spicy stews. Now modern science is backing its health benefits—and there's a lot to explore and love!

Fenugreek is a power spice in my pantry for several reasons: It is fiber rich, since about half the seed consists of both insoluble and soluble fiber, and it contains enough amino acids for researchers to suggest that its protein content may be close to that of soybeans. It's also packed with antioxidants and vitamins (A, $B_1$, $B_2$, $B_3$, and C).

.........................................................................................................

Fenugreek is sold in many forms: as a dried herb, as seeds, and as a fresh leafy vegetable. I mostly use the seed in its ground form. You only need a little—too much can be bitter!

**STUDIES SHOW THAT FENUGREEK MAY:**

Fight multiple forms of cancer—including breast, prostate, skin, and lung—by inhibiting tumor cell proliferation, killing suspicious and abnormal cells, and protecting your DNA

Reduce whole-body inflammation

Fight diabetes by helping lower blood sugar levels, restore pancreatic beta cells, and regulate insulin release

Decrease fat deposits in the liver

Ameliorate symptoms of painful menstrual cramps such as fatigue, headache, and lack of energy

Lower triglycerides and increase good cholesterol in your blood, while flushing out unnecessary cholesterol

Demonstrate antimicrobial activity against nasty bacterial infections

Help with weight loss by reducing hunger, regulating digestion, and flushing extra sugars out of the body before they enter the bloodstream

# Garlic

Fight cancer by inhibiting carcinogens, protecting healthy cells' DNA, suppressing tumor cell proliferation, and modulating the immune system

Support the cardiovascular system by lowering blood pressure, managing high cholesterol, and preventing hardening of the arteries

Dissolve blood clots, reducing the risk of heart attacks and strokes

Stimulate immune function and exhibit antimicrobial, antiviral, and antifungal properties, which may help prevent the common cold

Decrease the risk of developing diabetes by lowering blood sugar levels and decreasing insulin resistance

Promote weight loss (specifically by reducing fat mass), especially in individuals with nonalcoholic fatty liver disease

Lower the risk of dementia and Alzheimer's disease

Enhance the liver's ability to detoxify foreign compounds

Encourage the growth of favorable gut bacteria

Besides vampires and people on first dates, who doesn't love garlic? This wonderfully pungent and nutritionally powerful root vegetable originated in Asia thousands of years ago; today over 252,000 tons of garlic are grown every year in the United States alone. Both the National Cancer Institute and the American Institute of Cancer Research recognize garlic's anticancer properties.

To activate allicin, the powerful compound in garlic that helps accomplish these benefits and to make fresh garlic more nutritionally effective, chop or crush the cloves and let sit for 10 to 15 minutes before cooking. (I usually mince the cloves first, then chop whatever other ingredients I'm using.) But if you need a shortcut, garlic powder still packs quite a nutritional punch.

Garlic powder is also an excellent salt substitute. Sprinkle some on popcorn and roasted nuts to brighten the flavor without the sodium—and combine it with other spices for nutritional extra credit. I also recommend sprinkling garlic powder all over poultry and other meats before cooking. Here's why: Blackened, charred meats can release cancer-promoting chemicals, but studies show that adding garlic powder to meat prior to cooking may reduce levels of these carcinogens between 66 and 85 percent. Plus, garlic has been shown to reduce the DNA damage created by these cooked-meat carcinogens.

Garlic powder and granulated garlic are different types of dried garlic. Garlic powder has a finer consistency, and its texture resembles cornstarch—in order to prevent it from caking, manufacturers often add anticaking chemicals (yuck!). Granulated garlic has bigger grains and is less prone to forming clumps. You'll find me using granulated varieties more often due to its purity and reduced likelihood of clumping.

# Ginger

STUDIES SUGGEST
THAT GINGER MAY:

Sad but true: Most Americans eat ginger only when it's drowning in sugar—whether it's in gingerbread, gingersnaps, or ginger ale. But in China, where ginger originated thousands of years ago, this intense root is stir-fried, steamed, and even steeped in water to make tea—no sugar required, because it's good on its own.

Ginger has historically been used for relieving coughs, colds, and the flu, but modern science is finding it may do much more! Researchers have identified over sixty phytonutrients in ginger that are responsible for ginger's many benefits.

Reduce the risk of cancer by killing and preventing the spread of cancer cells

Promote weight loss by aiding digestion and suppressing fat cell creation

Alleviate nausea and vomiting caused by chemotherapy, surgery, pregnancy, or basic motion sickness

Relieve pain from menstrual cramping, heavy muscle workouts, rheumatism, or osteoarthritis

Prevent and heal stomach ulcers caused by stress, painkillers, alcohol, or *H. pylori* infection by strengthening the protective mucosal layer of your stomach

Increase the liver's detoxifying enzymes

Alleviate allergies by inhibiting histamine release

Reduce the risk of diabetes by lowering blood sugars, improving insulin signaling, and stimulating the enzyme that processes antioxidants

---

If you're buying fresh ginger, look for shiny, taut skin. It should be thin enough to nick with your fingernail—never thick and fibrous. Next, take a whiff. Is it pungent and spicy? If yes, your ginger is up to snuff. Avoid ginger with soft spots—it's been sitting on display way too long.  If you use ginger pretty frequently (two or three times a week), store it in the crisper drawer of your fridge in a resealable plastic bag with all the air removed. Otherwise, store it in your freezer and grate it whenever you need it.

I often simply simmer ginger in hot water to enjoy it after a meal to ease digestion. Ground ginger can be sprinkled on breakfasts as an anti-inflammatory and satiating boost.

# Nutmeg

Reduce inflammatory
processes and reduce the
risk of cancer

Maintain steady blood
sugar levels by enhancing
insulin sensitivity

Protect the liver from
damage due to its anti-
inflammatory effects

Mitigate weight gain on a
cellular level

Prevent flares of viral
diarrhea

Shuttle extra cholesterol
out of your body,
promoting cardiovascular
health

Enhance memory and
learning abilities, even in
the setting of Alzheimer's
disease

It's not just for holiday desserts. While you may know nutmeg for its flavorful role in pumpkin pie, eggnog, and custards, for hundreds of years it's also been used in a variety of savory dishes, including meats and stews. And you don't need a whole lot: Research shows that only a pinch of nutmeg used in cooking is enough to deliver significant anti-inflammatory effects.

Nutmeg's aroma is powerful, so you really only need a sprinkle (½ to ¼ teaspoon ground nutmeg) to pack a big flavor and anti-inflammatory punch! Keep to less than 1 tablespoon per day to avoid excess doses.

Here are a few of the many ways you can use this sweet spice:

**In meat-based dishes:** Nutmeg rounds out the flavor of lasagna, marinara sauces, and curries.

**In squashes:** It adds a delicate touch to winter squashes like acorn and butternut.

**In warm drinks:** Add nutmeg to chai, hot cider, or coffee.

**In holiday baking, of course:** Nutmeg pairs well with cinnamon, cardamom, and cloves. You really can't make a pumpkin pie without it!

# Nutritional Yeast

Nutritional yeast just might become as trendy as kale and kombucha. Not only does nutritional yeast have a nutty, cheesy flavor that makes it an ideal vegan sub for Parmesan cheese, but it also offers a wealth of health benefits—particularly in enhancing your immune system. Nutritional yeast is an inactive form of yeast that is produced by culturing and deactivating the yeast with heat so that it won't colonize in our bodies. Even though it's deactivated, nutritional yeast contains compounds called 1, 3–beta glucans, which give the immune system a boost by stimulating the body's natural defenses.

Nutritional yeast is a complete protein: a couple of spoonfuls of nutritional yeast adds 8 to 10 grams (depending on the brand) of protein to your dish—without excessive fat or carbs. It's also packed with other nutrients, including a full spectrum of B vitamins. That's why I call it a "vegan multivitamin"!

**STUDIES SHOW THAT NUTRITIONAL YEAST MAY:**

Strengthen the immune system and the body's natural defenses while reducing inflammation

Reduce chances of getting the common cold by up to 25 percent

Promote cellular energy production (and therefore boost midafternoon energy)

Support the metabolism of carbs, fats, and proteins

Help maintain a healthy nervous system

Promote strong and healthy hair, skin, and nails

Detoxify the body with the natural antioxidant selenium

Go for either nutritional yeast flakes or powder—they taste the same but have a slightly different texture. Since the B vitamins are sensitive to light, avoid buying nutritional yeast from a bulk bin and instead choose packages that are opaque. And if you're vegan, check the package to ensure that it's rich in vitamin $B_{12}$.

Use nutritional yeast to add an immune-boosting cheesy flavor to your dishes. Sprinkle on top of salads, soups, and pastas—any time you'd use a bit of Parmesan!

# Orange Peel

**STUDIES SHOW THAT
ORANGE PEEL MAY:**

Reduce the risk of
diabetes by normalizing
how the body metabolizes
sugars

Decrease blood pressure
by helping blood vessels
relax

Suppress appetite, helping
with weight control

Promote mental health
and reduce the risk
of Alzheimer's and
Parkinson's diseases

Decrease inflammation
in the airways, alleviating
allergic asthma

Soothe arthritis symptoms

Reduce anxiety

Protect the liver from
damage from toxins

Manage acid reflux

Fend off bacterial
infections

Everyone knows oranges are good for you, but most people toss the most nutritious part: the peel. Studies show that the orange peel is an even richer, more concentrated source of antioxidants than the pulp. I'm not just talking about vitamin C (though the peel does contain more of it than the fruit). Orange peel also contains powerful compounds such as hesperidin and d-Limonene, which exert powerful anti-inflammatory effects throughout your body and may also have cancer-fighting properties.

Grated orange peel makes a sweet substitute for lemon zest—it brightens up bean salads, dressings, pancake mixes, warm cereals, sweet potatoes, and smoothies. While fresh zest offers an unmistakable, refreshing zing to your dish, granulated dried orange peel provides a mild pop of flavor along with a dose of daily power when you don't have the fresh fruit around. You can easily find granulated orange peel in the spice aisle of most markets.

One of my favorite uses for orange peel is to make orange tea—no bag required. Simply drop some dried orange peels in hot water, then add some ginger or chai tea. If you're feeling congested, the steam will help clear out your sinuses. I also freely shake granulanted orange peel onto oatmeal and always add generous sprinkles into my smoothies for an extra dose of all-around goodness.

# Oregano

Oregano is ranked as the food with the second-highest concentration of antioxidants per gram (right behind cloves)—outperforming berries, leafy greens, and nuts. A little-known fact is that dried oregano has even more antioxidants than fresh oregano. In addition, oregano contains several bioactive components (such as cymene, quercetin, and rosmarinic acid) that work together on a chemical level to boost this herb's antioxidant, anti-inflammatory, and antimicrobial effects.

..................................................................................................

The origin of oregano can determine its flavor. For example, Mediterranean oregano is milder and sweeter than Mexican oregano (which has a darker, stronger, more robust flavor). Whichever you prefer, go for the dried herb for more antioxidants and a stronger flavor overall.

## STUDIES SHOW OREGANO MAY:

Selectively kill cancer cells, especially those related to breast and colon cancer

Boost gut health by decreasing inflammation and improving the integrity of the intestinal barrier

Lower LDL cholesterol and increase HDL cholesterol, reducing your risk of heart disease

Soothe digestive cramps by decreasing smooth muscle contractions in the intestines

Promote liver health due to antioxidant and anti-inflammatory effects

Balance blood sugars to help fight diabetes

Reduce risk of food spoilage and poisoning because of its potent antimicrobial activity

# Paprika

In the United States, we tend to think of paprika as a decorative sprinkle on deviled eggs, but I hope to change that by showing everyone what an amazing power spice paprika is, and how to use it in pretty much every savory dish.

Let's start with the source of the intense red: carotenoids. Paprika is made by grinding down capsicum peppers (sweet bell peppers), which are loaded with thirty-four kinds of carotenoids. Paprika's carotenoids include the well-known beta-carotene, lutein, and zeaxanthin, plus compounds such as capsanthin and capsorubin—found exclusively in paprika—that have been shown to reduce the chronic inflammation in our body caused by excess fat. Paprika also contains vitamin A (1 tablespoon has 66 percent of your daily recommended value!), which aids in vision and supports healthy cell development, and nutrients such as vitamin E, iron, and even fiber.

........................................................................

Depending on the variety of pepper used, paprika can range from mild to spicy in flavor and from bright red to brown in color. Most paprika sold in stores is pretty mild and is referred to as "sweet paprika" or just "paprika," but you can also purchase smoked paprika, which is made from peppers dried over a wood fire. Because paprika often has a mild flavor, you can liberally sprinkle it on top of a range of dishes for a bright pop of color. Cooking paprika also releases its full flavor profile and may help your body absorb many of the antioxidants.

# Parsley

Something that drives me crazy is seeing parsley used only as a decoration—especially when it's the healthiest item on a plate! I understand that it's a bitter herb, so I don't expect anyone to go to town on a parsley salad. But parsley is a true power herb: Its primary phytonutrient (apigenin) may kill cancer cells, prevent tumor cell invasion and metastasis, and inhibit a cancer cell's ability to take in glucose as fuel, thus stunting its growth. Parsley is also packed with vitamins C, A, and K as well as folate, iron, calcium, magnesium, potassium, and manganese. But it's not just a multivitamin.

You'll find two types of fresh parsley in grocery stores: curly leaf and flat leaf (also called Italian). Flat-leaf parsley has a stronger flavor, but both convey similar health benefits. You can store parsley for up to 1 week in the fridge. Dried parsley offers a concentrated source of apigenin—it's a nice shortcut when I don't have fresh around! You can add parsley (fresh or dried) to essentially any savory dish, including soups, stews, salads (particularly quinoa and bean salads), sandwiches, pasta, marinades, dressings, dips, and even smoothies.

**STUDIES SHOW THAT PARSLEY MAY:**

Debloat your belly by acting as a diuretic and flushing excess water out of the body

Lower blood sugar levels to fight diabetes

Reduce inflammation and oxidative stress in brain cells

Ease digestive cramps and irritable bowels by relaxing contractions in the small intestine

Reduce bad breath (sounds trivial, but who doesn't want that?)

# Rosemary

**STUDIES SHOW THAT
ROSEMARY MAY:**

Prevent cancer cell and tumor proliferation and specifically reduce the risk of breast cancer

Improve cognitive function—a mere teaspoon was shown to improve memory speed

Help with weight loss by preventing fat cell creation and increasing fat excretion in the stool

Protect the liver by restoring antioxidant enzymes and reducing inflammatory cells

Promote heart health by lowering inflammation in the arteries

Ameliorate memory deficits and neuronal degeneration, lowering the risk of Alzheimer's disease

Debloat your tummy due to its diuretic effects

Improve blood sugar levels

This herb, often a staple in Italian cooking, boasts a powerful fragrance that enhances the flavor of your dishes and improves your health. Rosemary leaves contain an essential oil rich in organic acids (carnosic, rosmarinic, and ursolic acids) that work together synergistically on a cellular level to magnify their antioxidant and anti-inflammatory effects. In other words, Mother Nature brilliantly combined these compounds to form one super herb—yet another example of why you should get your nutrients from foods and not extracts or pills!

Both fresh rosemary sprigs as well as the dried herb provide a woodsy, pine-like fragrance that pairs wonderfully with almost any meat or vegetable dish, especially roasted potatoes.

# Saffron

For centuries, saffron has been a symbol of wealth, as it is easily the world's most expensive spice by weight, since it must be harvested by hand from delicate flowers that bloom just one week a year. One gram of dry saffron takes about 150 flowers. That's one serious bouquet! Last I checked, it was running about $10 per gram (real gold, by contrast, is about $40 per gram). But it's worth it, because saffron is rich in chemical compounds that give you a wealth of health benefits.

When it comes to carotenoids (red- and orange-colored antioxidants), saffron makes carrots and tomatoes look like wannabes. In addition to packing in beta-carotene, lycopene, and zeaxanthin, saffron includes unique phytochemicals such as crocetin, crocin, and safranal, all of which may be the secret behind saffron's health benefits.

Saffron powder loses its flavor quickly, so when possible, buy whole threads and store them in an airtight container away from sunlight. Take out only what you need and crumble the threads before using.

Beware: The market is flooded with fakes. If you see a packet of saffron for just a few dollars, put it back. To ensure you get true, high-quality saffron, make sure it comes from Iran or Spain, as these countries produce 80 percent of the world's supply. Look for fine, uniform, red trumpet-shaped threads with a thin yellow tendril on one side. After you bring it home, place it in water for a few minutes and see if the threads retain their individual color and if the water turns a honey-yellow. If all the color washes out of the threads, you've caught a fake.

Saffron classically appears in rice dishes such as risotto, pilafs, and paella, but I like to use it to give any whole grain a power-boost.

## STUDIES SHOW THAT SAFFRON MAY:

Enhance your mood with antidepression effects, ease anxiety and insomnia, and boost memory

Reduce the desire to snack—especially stress or emotional eating

Maintain healthy blood vessels by reducing cholesterol levels and preventing plaque deposits

Lead to better glucose control and decrease risk of diabetes by reducing blood sugar levels and stimulating insulin release

Prevent gastric ulcers

Protect the liver by acting as an antioxidant, reducing inflammation, and enhancing the body's natural antioxidant defense systems

Soothe symptoms of premenstrual syndrome (PMS)

Inhibit cancer cell proliferation and modulate the immune system to fight off colorectal, liver, pancreatic, and lung cancer cells

Act as an effective therapy for Alzheimer's disease

# Sumac

Inhibit cancer cell growth
and kill already existent
cancer cells

Reduce the risk of
cardiovascular disease

Lower post-meal blood
sugar levels, causing an
antidiabetic effect

Decrease systemic
inflammation

Promote liver health by
exerting antioxidant
effects on liver cells

Exhibit broad antibacterial
properties

Attenuate bone loss
in postmenopausal
osteoporosis

Soothe an upset stomach

If you, like most people in the States, are just now discovering sumac, time to add it to your power pantry! Sumac provides a tangy, earthy flavor that's less tart yet more complex than something like lemon juice. It's one of the main components of za'atar, but it also adds a bright red color when added to any dish on its own. Sumac has a greater antioxidant content than black pepper, red pepper, fennel, cardamom, turmeric, white mustard, and nutmeg. That's not to say the others aren't potent—but sumac towers above them.

Ground sumac is readily available in Middle Eastern markets and online, but it's slowly making its way to general grocery stores.

I always have a jar of ground sumac on my kitchen table so I can add sprinkles of its earthy, lemony flavor on just about any food. Dust it over salad, poached eggs, baked sweet potatoes, roasted vegetables, popcorn, or hummus (page 138) to add flavor complexity. If you need a citrusy flavor without the acidic juice—such as in a dry rub or marinade—sumac is a great option.

# Thyme

If you're like me, you probably knew about thyme long before you ever tasted it. (I blame a certain Simon & Garfunkel song.) Well, wait till you hear what it does for your health! The compound that gives thyme its name and distinctive scent is thymol, a potential source of both anti-inflammatory and anticancer properties.

..................................................................................................

Although thyme is part of the summer harvest, supermarkets sell it year-round, either fresh or dried. Fresh tastes best, of course, but it must be used quickly (usually within a week); however, you can certainly freeze fresh thyme for later use. Dried thyme is also a great option—like oregano, it retains most of its flavor (and nutrition!) when dried.

**STUDIES SHOW THAT THYME MAY:**

Halt tumor cell proliferation

Boost enzymes that metabolize carcinogens before they can do any damage

Provide antibacterial and antifungal effects (it's used as a natural food preservative, and thymol is a key ingredient in some mouthwashes and all-natural hand sanitizers)

Boost the body's natural antioxidant enzymes in the liver

Decrease total cholesterol levels, even in a high-fat diet

Increase the amount of healthy "brown fat" in the body. This type of fat has been shown to boost metabolism by burning off extra energy as heat

Boost your mood by increasing levels of the neurotransmitters dopamine and serotonin

Reduce pain associated with inflammation

Lower blood pressure

# Turmeric

Prevent cancer cell growth, kill tumor cells, and inhibit gene expression associated with cancer development

Boost your body's natural antioxidant enzymes and directly remove cell-damaging free radicals

Greatly reduce oxidative stress and inflammation in the digestive system, alleviating inflammatory bowel disease, colitis, chronic pancreatitis, and stomach ulcers

Improve carbohydrate and fat metabolism

Suppress fat accumulation by decreasing the number and size of fat cells

Reduce blood sugar levels to combat diabetes

Increase the liver's natural detox enzymes and protect it from damage

Protect the brain from Alzheimer's and Parkinson's diseases

Alleviate symptoms of asthma by reducing inflammation in the respiratory system

Ameliorate autoimmune diseases including multiple sclerosis, rheumatoid arthritis, and psoriasis, due to its anti-inflammatory effects

Though turmeric has been cultivated for five thousand years, most Americans are only now discovering this must-have power spice. Over 1,700 laboratory studies have shown turmeric may potentially curb obesity, reduce diabetes, protect against cardiovascular disease, and fight cancer. The key component behind turmeric's nutritional power is curcumin, an extremely powerful antioxidant and anti-inflammatory compound.

Fresh turmeric root looks like ginger on the outside, but the inside is bright orange. Store the root in the fridge and grate it prior to use—just be careful because it tends to stain! On a daily basis, I gravitate toward organic turmeric powder for ease.

The big catch with turmeric is its relatively low level of bioavailability, meaning your body doesn't easily absorb and utilize curcumin. Here are some tips to help boost its bioavailability:

**Just add black pepper!** Studies show that a mere $\frac{1}{8}$ teaspoon of black pepper can increase curcumin's bioavailability by 2,000 percent.

**Eat turmeric with veggies that contain quercetin.** These include red-leaf lettuce, kale, asparagus, romaine lettuce, bell peppers, snap peas, broccoli, onions, and capers.

**Add turmeric to healthy fats (olive oil, avocado, nuts), as curcumin is naturally fat soluble.** Sprinkle some on nuts prior to toasting, or add it to avocado toast and salad dressings.

**Sprinkle turmeric over fish.** Curcumin and the omega-3s in fish fight breast cancer more effectively together than separately.

**Heating turmeric increases its solubility, which may enhance its bioavailability.** So turmeric is a perfect fit for warm drinks and soups.

# Power Couples and Trios (and More)

One spice is nice, but combine multiple spices together and you get so much more!

Numerous studies have revealed that spices acting together may boost each other's nutritional effects on a cellular level. There are three main categories of how spices interact. Some spices increase the ability for another spice to be absorbed by the body. Some synergistically interact to supercharge chemical reactions. And some combinations provide a double dose of a particularly potent phytonutrient.

Let's look at how to mix and match spices to maximize their benefits—and feel free to experiment with combos of your own.

## 1. Absorption Enhancers

What's the point of spicing if the compounds aren't optimally absorbed into your cells, where they can really make a difference in your health? That would be like pumping gas into a car that has a hole in its tank. These are my favorite combinations of spices that research has shown may boost absorption, bioavailability, and therefore utilization of the beneficial compounds in these spices:

**CACAO + MATCHA**

**CACAO + TURMERIC**

**TURMERIC + PARSLEY**

Black pepper is the ultimate sidekick in several more beneficial pairings. It increases the bioavailability of a myriad of nutrients by boosting our body's digestive and transportation enzymes, increasing blood flow to the gastrointestinal tract to help absorb nutrients, and slowing the breakdown and elimination of some healthy compounds. Scientists are finding that it may only take about ⅛ teaspoon of ground black pepper to yield these effects.

**BLACK PEPPER + BASIL**

**BLACK PEPPER + CAYENNE**

**BLACK PEPPER + MATCHA**

**BLACK PEPPER + PAPRIKA**

**BLACK PEPPER + TURMERIC**

## 2. Synergistic Action

Certain chemicals in spices and herbs have amazing synergistic properties: They may boost each other's actions on a cellular level, whether it's antioxidant, anti-inflammatory, or disease-fighting effects.

**CACAO + TURMERIC =**
stronger inhibition of cancer cell growth

**CACAO + CAYENNE =**
promote cancer cell death

**CAYENNE + MATCHA =**
ten times greater inhibition of cancer cell growth

**GINGER + CINNAMON + MATCHA =**
regulate glucose levels to lower the risk of diabetes

**CUMIN + CORIANDER =**
increased antioxidant and antimicrobial activities

**GARLIC + FENUGREEK =**
augmented antioxidant effect

**ROSEMARY + TURMERIC =**
fight leukemia

**OREGANO + BASIL + THYME =**
synergistic antimicrobial effect

**CUMIN + THYME =**
boosted antibacterial properties

**CARDAMOM + TURMERIC =**
prevent stomach ulcers

## 3. Double Dose

Certain health-boosting nutrients are found in multiple spices, so you can double up on the flavor *and* the benefits. Other compounds work toward the same goal possibly via different chemical pathways. I say, let's power up our meals from multiple angles!

**GINGER + CINNAMON + CARDAMOM + SAFFRON =**
promote a healthy heart

**BASIL + ROSEMARY + THYME =**
improve heart health

**GARLIC + TURMERIC =**
lower the risk of heart disease

**GARLIC + GINGER + CAYENNE =**
decrease cholesterol levels

**GARLIC + ONION =**
reduce the risk of cancer

**PAPRIKA + CAYENNE =**
concentrated antioxidant and anti-inflammatory benefits

**SAFFRON + TURMERIC + BLACK PEPPER =**
decrease the risk of Alzheimer's disease

**TURMERIC + FENUGREEK =**
lower cholesterol levels

# Bonus: Power Up with Food Synergism!

Spices don't just boost each other's powers; an individual spice can boost the nutrition of other foods as well. Here are a few combinations that stand out in their health-promoting abilities.

**BLACK PEPPER = absorption booster**

Grind pepper on basically everything to enhance the benefits of not just other spices but also the nutrients in your everyday foods. Use it to season foods that are rich in the following nutrients:

- **BETA-CAROTENE:** broccoli, carrots, kale, spinach, sweet potatoes, winter squash
- **COENZYME Q10:** fish, meats, broccoli, cauliflower, peanuts, pistachios, sesame seeds
- **IRON:** beans, edamame, flaxseeds, hempseeds, leafy greens, lentils, nuts, potatoes, pumpkin, sesame, tofu
- **MAGNESIUM:** almonds, avocado, black beans, chard, pumpkin seeds, spinach
- **RESVERATROL:** blueberries, cacao, peanuts, pistachios, red wine, cranberries (finish off a peppery meal with one of these!)
- **SELENIUM:** Brazil nuts, eggs, fish, seafood, spinach

**CAYENNE + CRUCIFEROUS VEGGIES =**
increased cancer-fighting properties

**CAYENNE + PEANUTS OR PISTACHIOS =**
seasoned nuts with a cancer-fighting kick

**GARLIC + ONIONS + FIBER-RICH VEGETABLES =**
upgraded anticancer effects

**GINGER + CINNAMON + COFFEE =**
synergistic antioxidant effects

**OREGANO + EXTRA-VIRGIN OLIVE OIL =**
longer-lasting oil with an antioxidant boost

**BASIL + ROSEMARY + THYME + TOMATOES =**
antioxidant powerhouse

**BASIL, ROSEMARY, OR THYME + VITAMIN E–RICH FOODS (SUCH AS OLIVE OIL, ALMONDS, SPINACH, AVOCADO, AND SWEET POTATO) =**
synergistic antioxidant effects

**ROSEMARY + GARLIC + TOMATOES =**
synergistic antioxidant power

**TURMERIC + QUERCETIN-RICH FOODS (SUCH AS CITRUS, DARK RED AND BLUE FRUITS, LEAFY GREENS, AND ONIONS) =**
increased absorption of curcumin, turmeric's main anti-inflammatory and disease-fighting compound

**TURMERIC + HEALTHY FATS =**
increased bioavailability of curcumin

**TURMERIC + OMEGA-3-RICH FISH =**
super-effective cancer fighter

# Outside the Spice Cabinet

## Ingredients

### Non-dairy Milk

#### SOY MILK

Soy milk has the most protein (7 grams per serving) compared with other alternative milks (1 to 4 grams per serving). Opt for an organic variety to avoid genetically modified and highly sprayed soybeans.

#### ALMOND MILK

Arguably the most popular milk alternative, almond milk is low in fat and calories and has a mild flavor—slightly sweet and nutty. It's versatile and can easily be used in smoothies and oatmeal.

#### CASHEW MILK

Cashew milk is creamier, less nutty, and a bit sweeter than almond milk.

#### COCONUT MILK

With a creamy consistency and sweet, coconut flavor, coconut milk is excellent in savory dishes like curry, stews, and soups, but it also adds a rich flavor to smoothies or hot cereal. Compared to other plant-based milks, it's higher in saturated fat—which you don't need much of in your diet.

#### RICE MILK

This is a good option for people with nut allergies; however, it's higher in carbohydrates (and often sugar) and lower in protein compared with other alternative milks.

#### FLAX MILK

Thin and smooth, flax milk contains anti-inflammatory omega-3 fatty acids, which have been linked to a lower risk of heart disease.

#### HEMP MILK

Similar to flax milk aside from its slightly nuttier flavor, hemp milk is thin and also contains omega-3 fatty acids.

#### OAT MILK

Super creamy and rich, oat milk tastes amazing in lattes (including turmeric lattes). Since it's made from a grain, it has a higher carbohydrate content than nut milks.

*To make your own hemp milk, blend ½ cup hempseeds and 3 cups water in a high-speed blender. You can add ½ teaspoon pure vanilla extract and ⅛ teaspoon ground cinnamon for flavor (I always do). Transfer to an airtight container and store in the refrigerator for up to 5 days.*

Once you've settled on what type of milk to buy, flip the carton around and check out the ingredient label. Avoid the following:

▶ **Added sugars** (often under the label of evaporated cane juice, cane sugar, or cane syrup)

▶ **Xanthan gum and guar gum** (emulsifiers that some people find difficult to digest, with resulting bloating or cramping)

▶ **Carrageenan** (a seaweed-based emulsifier that has also been linked to inflammation and intestinal ulcerations and tumors)

▶ **Vegetable oils** (canola oil, corn oil, safflower oil, sunflower seed oil, or soybean oil—all of which are pro-inflammatory)

You may also opt to make your own nut milk—note that it will not be fortified with calcium or other nutrients:

*Place 2 cups raw almonds or cashews in a bowl and cover them with filtered water. Soak overnight. The next day, rinse them thoroughly with cold running water, then drain. Place the nuts in a high-powered blender along with 6 cups filtered water (you may add ½ teaspoon ground cinnamon and 1 teaspoon pure vanilla extract for flavor) and blend on high speed for 1 to 2 minutes, until frothy. Strain the mixture through cheesecloth or a nut-milk bag, squeezing it to extract as much liquid as possible. Store in an air-tight container in the refrigerator for up to 3 days.*

## Oil

You want to choose the right type of oil—ditch the pro-inflammatory corn, canola, safflower, and soybean oil. Here are my top picks for anti-inflammatory oils and when to use each.

### COLD-PRESSED (UNREFINED) EXTRA-VIRGIN OLIVE OIL

Cold-pressed extra-virgin olive oil is flavorful and has a low smoke point. It's gently pressed and minimally processed, thus retaining at least thirty plant-based chemicals that account for its antioxidant, anti-inflammatory, and potential anticancer effects. Don't heat it up—drizzle it over cold dishes, like salads.

### EXTRA-VIRGIN (REFINED) OLIVE OIL

Although less flavorful than cold-pressed olive oil, the refining process gives this oil a higher smoke point (meaning you can heat it up and use in cooking). This should be your staple oil for medium-heat sautéing and braising veggies.

### AVOCADO OIL

Avocado oil adds a buttery flavor to foods and has a very high smoke point. It's also rich in heart-healthy monounsaturated fats and anti-inflammatory compounds. It's best for high-heat cooking, baking, and searing.

### WALNUT OIL

Walnut oil provides a rich, nutty flavor and is high in omega-3 fatty acids, which are highly anti-inflammatory and help reduce cancer risk. Drizzle it over cold dishes, salads, or gently sautéed vegetables to add a more complex flavor.

## Salt

I don't want you to rely on salt for flavoring—spices bring a colorful range of flavors to the table—but sometimes a pinch can perk up a dish.

I primarily use sea salt (as opposed to kosher salt) in my cooking. Sea salt is made from evaporating seawater and can contain trace amounts of minerals like potassium, iron, and zinc. Because sea salt has a larger grain and is less refined than table salt, it creates a more powerful burst of flavor when sprinkled on top of your food, so you tend to need less salt when using sea salt. I also use Himalayan pink salt, which contains trace amounts of calcium, iron, potassium, and magnesium, with slightly lower amounts of sodium compared with table salt. The pink color makes it a great finishing salt—but I reach for it all the time in cooking and use it interchangeably with sea salt.

Regular table salt (e.g., Morton's) is heavily processed to create a uniform grain, and usually contains an additive to prevent caking. It's also easy to oversalt food with this type, as one pinch contains *a lot* of salt crystals. I don't use this often.

## Sweeteners

Sweeteners—whether natural or sugar substitutes—tend to make you crave more intense sweet flavors. The best thing to do is to train your taste buds to need only a little bit of sweetness. But when the time is right, here are some to reach for—in moderation.

### DATES

They're among the sweetest fruits around—so just one goes a long way in delivering a punch of sweet flavor, along with vitamins, minerals, and fiber for balance.

### HONEY

Darker honey contains more vitamins and trace minerals than the lighter ones. It also contains antioxidants than may lower blood pressure and improve your cholesterol. I like using minimally processed, raw honey because it has up to four times more antioxidants compared with the commercial processed variety, as well as higher amounts of antimicrobial and health-boosting compounds. Children under 1 year, pregnant women, and immunocompromised individuals should avoid raw honey. You may also see manuka honey, which is sourced from a special plant native to New Zealand, which has a stronger, deeper flavor.

### MAPLE SYRUP

"Grade A, Dark Color Robust Flavor" is my favorite type of maple syrup because it packs a big flavor punch, so you can use less and still get the sweetness you crave in a totally all-natural form. It's still sugar, but it has a leg up on refined sugar because it's relatively unprocessed and contains some naturally occurring minerals.

## Beans

I use legumes liberally in my recipes. While it's best (and most cost-effective) to soak and cook dried beans from scratch (see opposite page), sometimes you're in a pinch and need a quick option. I tell my clients to leave most cans on the shelf, because they tend to be contaminated with the chemical bisphenol A (BPA). Choosing BPA- and BPS-free containers is one way to reduce the risk of a potentially big health concern. Eden Foods' cans do not contain either chemical. I've also found that the BPA- and BPS-free Tetra Paks are a safe container for beans (as well as plant-based milks and broth).

## Sprouted Organic Tofu

Soy can be a controversial topic in the nutrition world, but I'm here to tell you it's okay—if you choose the right types. You may have heard the claim that soy can lead to breast cancer because it contains hormones, but this simply isn't true. Soy does contain phytoestrogens or plant hormones that are similar in structure to human estrogen. While high levels of human estrogen may lead to breast cancer, soy phytoestrogens actually have an antiestrogenic, anticancer effect. Studies have concluded that a high intake of whole soy foods is linked to lower risk of breast cancer incidence, recurrence, and mortality. Let me repeat that—whole soy foods do not cause cancer; rather, they reduce the risk of cancer.

The American Cancer Society and the American Institute for Cancer Research encourage eating two or three servings of whole soy foods per week for its health benefits. Choosing organic soy is important, as soy is a highly sprayed and genetically modified crop. And I always recommend sprouted varieties, as it makes some nutrients more bioavailable and the tofu more easily digestible. Sprouted organic tofu is readily available at health food stores and is comparable to organic tofu in terms of price.

### HOW TO COOK ANY BEANS

Prepared beans are a great shortcut, but did you know that home-cooked beans are about 80 percent cheaper? Here's my quick and easy guide to prepping your own legumes at home—remember that 1 pound of dried beans equals 5 cups cooked.

**Clean:** Rinse the beans and discard the rinse water.

**Soak:** Soak the beans for 4 to 6 hours (I usually soak them overnight for convenience) in a pot or large bowl filled with filtered water.

**Add water:** Drain the beans, put them in a large pot, and cover with more water—enough to cover the beans by about 2 inches.

**Flavor:** Toss in some goodness! I like to add onion, garlic, bay leaves, and a few slices of fresh ginger or fennel.

**Cook:** Bring the water to a boil over medium-high heat and skim off any foam. Reduce the heat to low and simmer with the lid off for the remaining cooking time. (The one exception is kidney beans, which must be boiled for 10 minutes first, then simmered.) You'll know they're done when the beans are tender and can be easily pierced or mashed.

Approximate Cooking Times:

**Black, cannellini, and azuki beans:** 45 to 60 minutes

**Kidney, navy, and pinto beans:** 1 to 1½ hours

**Garbanzo beans:** 1½ to 2½ hours

**Season:** Season to taste with sea salt or Himalayan salt, freshly ground black pepper, and any spices you like (I love using cumin and paprika). Finish off with a drizzle of olive oil.

# Whole Grains

Whole grains contain all the components of the grain (the bran, germ, and endosperm). They're relatively unprocessed and contain greater amounts of fiber, B vitamins, iron, and magnesium compared to refined grains. I include a wide range of whole grains in my diet.

### OATS

Oats are quick to whip together—and they make a great base for spices. They are rich in beta-glucans, a type of soluble fiber that has been shown to reduce cholesterol, stabilize blood sugar levels, boost the immune system, and even fight cancer. Oats are naturally gluten-free (but can be contaminated with gluten from other grains, so if you adhere to a gluten-free diet, choose some that are certified gluten-free). I prefer to purchase organic oats to limit the amount of contamination.

▶ Steel-cut oats are the least processed type—they're chewy and hearty, and contain slightly more fiber than the other varieties of oats. They take about 30 minutes to cook on the stovetop, but you can also use a pressure cooker for a quicker cook time.

▶ Rolled oats are steamed, then pressed during processing, which results in a shorter cook time (2 to 5 minutes on the stovetop).

▶ Quick-cook (or instant) oats are the most processed type. They cook within a few minutes and tend to make a soft, mushy porridge. I tend to avoid quick-cook oats because they have a higher glycemic index and can cause spikes in blood sugars.

### QUINOA

This ancient grain is high in protein, is a complete protein (meaning it contains all the essential amino acids), is moderately high in fiber, and cooks quickly (about 10 to 12 minutes on the stovetop). Red quinoa holds its shape the best and is great in salads; black is a bit nuttier and sweeter; and white has the most delicate texture.

### SORGHUM

Originally hailing from Africa, this chewy yet light grain takes on whatever flavor you provide. You can cook it up as a porridge, prepare it al dente and add to salads, or pop the kernels into a snack that resembles mini popcorn.

### RICE

Opt for brown over white rice, as it's higher in fiber and minerals. Wild rice has a slightly nutty flavor, is also rich in fiber, and additionally contains antioxidants. Purple rice has a sticky texture and contains anthocyanins—a unique antioxidant that may have anti-inflammatory and anticancer properties.

## Matcha

When you steep green tea, only about five percent of the nutrients end up in the cup! Matcha is distinct from other types of green tea because, rather than just steeping the leaves in hot water, the leaves themselves are ground into a fine powder. By actually drinking the powdered leaves, you're getting the full power of the polyphenols—compounds with major antioxidant properties and potential weight loss benefits.

The key is buying high-quality, 100-percent matcha, so read the packaging carefully. If it's called just "powdered green tea," it's likely low quality. Choose ceremonial matcha as opposed to cooking-grade matcha. The best matcha leaves come from Japan, not China. Once you open the package, the matcha powder should be a vibrant green color (not dull or yellowish) with a fine, silky texture. My personal favorites include DōMatcha, AOI Matcha, and Art of Tea.

Tip: *Avoid adding cow's milk to matcha, as proteins and fat from cow's milk bind with EGCG, making it less bioavailable. The same effect has not been shown to occur with alternative milks.*

## Granulated Onion

Similarly to garlic, dried onion exists as granulated particles and as fine powder. Granulated onion is more flavorful and generally preferable over onion powder, which can be filled with anticaking compounds.

## Pure Vanilla Extract

What's the difference between pure vanilla extract, vanilla flavoring, and imitation vanilla? Imitation vanilla is made from artificial flavorings, often from chemical-containing wood by-products, and tends to have a harsh, slightly bitter aftertaste. Vanilla flavoring is usually a combination of imitation vanilla and pure vanilla extract. It's cheap, but still has some synthetic ingredients. Pure vanilla extract is a bit more pricey, but it's worth it to ensure you're getting true, natural vanilla as well as a richer, deeper vanilla flavor. Some brands contain corn syrup or caramel color—try to avoid these and stick to a brand that has a small amount of cane sugar (the sugar softens the aroma). Store in a cool, dark place for 6 to 12 months.

# Power Up Everyday Foods

Some pre-packaged products contain spices, but barely enough to make a difference, and they almost never in the synergistic combos that take nutrition to the next level. Here are some products found on most shopping lists, and the few pinches of spices that will take them from average to amazing.

## MARINARA SAUCE

Cooked tomatoes are much better for you than raw ones. The heat and healthy fats (olive oil) make tomato's powerful nutrients easier for your body to absorb. When you buy marinara sauce, make sure it's organic and contains no added sugar. Then stir in ¼ teaspoon each of thyme, rosemary, and crushed red pepper flakes, plus 1 teaspoon each of parsley, oregano, and basil (all dried).

## NUT BUTTER

Stir 1 to 2 tablespoons of either cacao, cacao plus cayenne, Golden Power Breakfast Blend (page 52), CinnaPeel Breakfast Blend (page 52), or Sweet Success Morning Power Blend (page 53) into a jar of nut butter (or sprinkle a spoonful on top of spread nut butter).

## HUMMUS

Stir in (or sprinkle on top) a teaspoon of the following: paprika, za'atar, Veggie Power-Up Blend (page 52), Everything Savory Power Blend (page 52), Moroccan Roll Blend (page 53), sumac, turmeric, or saffron (soak ½ teaspoon crushed saffron threads in 1 tablespoon warm water for 5 minutes, then stir in the saffron and water mixture).

## COFFEE

Stir in ¼ teaspoon of cinnamon, a pinch of cardamom, a pinch of cloves, and unsweetened non-dairy milk. Or try adding a pinch of ground ginger for a spicy twist.

## POPCORN OR POPPED SORGHUM

Make movie night even more magical by shaking generous amounts of cinnamon, nutritional yeast, cayenne, or any of the spice blends on pages 52–53 on top.

## EGGS

Add a sprinkle of za'atar, cumin, or paprika, or use a pinch of the Everything Savory Power Blend (page 52). You can also try serving them scrambled with Chimichurri Sauce (page 134).

## GRAINS

Whatever your preferred grain, you can turn bland into grand by adding saffron. Simply grind 7 to 10 saffron threads in a small bowl using the back of a spoon. Add 1 tablespoon of hot water, mix evenly, and let sit for 5 minutes. Pour the saffron-water into a pot with the raw grain and water, then cook as you normally would.

## HONEY

I always keep a jar on hand of what I refer to as "Immune Boosting Honey Bomb" for a quick and easy tea. To make it: Place ½ cup of honey in a jar and add 1 teaspoon each of ground ginger and turmeric along with ½ teaspoon of black pepper. Stir well. Store in an airtight sealed jar for up to 1 month. I stir ½ to 1 teaspoon of this mixture into a cup of hot water or tea to enjoy its immune-boosting perks!

# About the Recipes

## Primarily Plant-Based

Through my years of research, I've come to the conclusion that a primarily plant-based diet is the most beneficial for your health. This aligns with the American Institute for Cancer Research's primarily plant-based diet recommendations, and the American Cancer Society's statement that a diet rich in plant-based foods may reduce the risk of cancer. Research also supports a plant-based diet for the prevention and treatment of heart disease and diabetes.

I encourage my clients to eat plant-based proteins because of their cancer and disease–fighting advantages over animal proteins. The most important idea for you to grasp regardless of your food philosophy is that you should really be packing plants—and spices, of course—into every meal. So, throughout this book you will see a sprinkle of dishes that include animal products such as fish, grass-fed meat, and organic chicken, but the dishes are heavy on plants such as vegetables, fruits, legumes, and whole grains. You'll see recipes that classify as vegan (v), or as vegan-option (vo), when easy ingredient swaps can make the dish vegan. Many are also gluten-free (GF).

## Choosing Organic

When it comes to your health, I believe that it's worth investing in organic foods. Research suggests that some organic fruits and vegetables contain up to 40 percent higher levels of antioxidants and have more trace minerals. The following fruits and vegetables are prone to having higher levels of pesticide contamination when conventionally grown, so I recommend you opt for their organic counterparts whenever possible:

- Apples
- Bell peppers
- Blueberries
- Celery
- Cucumbers
- Grapes
- Hot peppers
- Kale and collard greens
- Nectarines
- Peaches
- Potatoes
- Snap peas
- Spinach
- Strawberries
- Tomatoes

On the flip side, these foods are lowest when it comes to pesticide load, so conventional is okay:

- Asparagus
- Avocados
- Cabbage
- Cantaloupe
- Cauliflower
- Eggplant
- Grapefruit
- Kiwi
- Mangoes
- Onions
- Papayas
- Pineapples
- Sweet corn
- Sweet peas
- Sweet potatoes

## Minimal Dairy

I personally don't eat dairy, and I encourage my clients to either eliminate or keep dairy consumption to a minimum due to its hormone content (see non-dairy alternatives on page 42).

# DIY Spice Blends

**Yes, you can buy ready-made spice blends at the supermarket.** They're convenient ... and expensive ... and filled with added junk like salt, sugar, color enhancers, and anticaking additives. You're better off putting together your own spice blends at home! Here's the scoop—make that multiple scoops: Creating your own blends is easy, and you'll always have them on hand for cooking, sprinkling, and even bringing to restaurants (as I do). They'll be far more pure and potent than the supermarket blends, and you can make as much or as little as you need for 6 months. Each of these blends has been carefully formulated to capitalize on powerful spice synergism.

Of course, if you're really, really busy and find that sourcing organic spices is too much of a hassle, you can always try Rachel Beller's Power Pantry line of spice blends—the same as the ones in these pages. But why not put your sourcing and mixing skills to the test first?

For each of these recipes, the only step is to whisk together and store the blend in a small tightly sealed container or jar (hooray for reusing!).

# CinnaPeel Breakfast Blend

(V) (GF)

My go-to breakfast blend—but don't limit it to just the morning! This unique trio of spices may work to balance blood sugars, and the orange peel in particular provides anti-cancer properties.

**6 tablespoons** ground cinnamon
**1 tablespoon** granulated orange peel
**¾ teaspoon** ground ginger

**POTENTIAL BENEFITS**
- Regulates blood sugars
- Fights cancer
- Counteracts weight gain
- Reduces sugar cravings

# Golden Power Breakfast Blend

(V) (GF)

Here I've combined four major anti-inflammatory spices. Cacao and turmeric may work together to fight cancer (plus cacao boosts turmeric absorption), and ginger and cinnamon can boost each other's anti-inflammatory effects.

**2 tablespoons** ground cinnamon
**2 tablespoons** cacao powder
**2 teaspoons** ground turmeric
**½ teaspoon** ground ginger

**POTENTIAL BENEFITS**
- Decreases inflammation
- Fights cancer
- Regulates blood sugars

# Everything Savory Power Blend

(V) (GF)

This flavorful blend gives anything savory an anti-cancer boost. Plus paprika is a powerful antioxidant, cumin and cayenne may help you lose weight, and turmeric and garlic have combined heart health benefits—black pepper helps boost this effect by 2,000 percent.

**5 tablespoons** paprika
**2 tablespoons** granulated garlic
**1½ tablespoons** ground turmeric
**1 tablespoon** ground cumin
**½ teaspoon** freshly ground black pepper
**½ teaspoon** cayenne (optional)

**POTENTIAL BENEFITS**
- Boosts antioxidant levels
- Assists with weight loss
- Lowers heart disease risk
- Fights cancer

# Veggie Power-Up Blend

(V) (GF)

Here's my specially formulated breast-cancer-protective blend. Turmeric's anti-cancer benefits are optimized with black pepper, parsley may prevent cancer cell growth, and garlic and onion may lower the risk of cancer. It's amazing on vegetables—and just about any dish!

**2 tablespoons** granulated garlic
**2 tablespoons** granulated onion
**2 tablespoons** ground turmeric
**1 tablespoon** dried parsley or cilantro
**1 teaspoon** freshly ground black pepper

## POTENTIAL BENEFITS

- Fights breast cancer
- Boosts immune function
- Decreases inflammation

## Moroccan Roll Blend

(V) (GF)

This savory-spicy-sweet blend will upgrade vegetable, legume, and protein dishes so they'll rock your system in so many ways! The spices synergistically work together to boost digestion and nutrient absorption.

**2 tablespoons** ground cumin
**1 tablespoon plus 1 teaspoon** ground turmeric
**1 tablespoon plus 1 teaspoon** ground cinnamon
**1 tablespoon plus 1 teaspoon** paprika
**2 teaspoons** cayenne
**1 teaspoon** freshly ground black pepper

## POTENTIAL BENEFITS

- Improves digestion
- Assists with weight loss
- Reduces risk of stomach ulcers

## Sweet Success Morning Power Blend

(V) (GF)

This adds a warm, spicy-sweet depth (think apple pie!) to your breakfasts, smoothies, and snacks. Ginger, nutmeg, and cloves may enhance liver function; cinnamon, allspice, and nutmeg can support brain power; and all the spices help balance blood sugars!

**¼ cup plus 2 tablespoons** ground cinnamon
**1½ teaspoons** ground ginger
**2 teaspoons** ground nutmeg
**½ teaspoon** ground allspice
**¼ teaspoon** ground cloves

## POTENTIAL BENEFITS

- Promotes liver health and helps with detoxification
- Reduces stress and enhances memory
- Regulates blood sugars

## Tex-Mex Power Blend

(V) (GF)

This antioxidant-rich blend is more savory than spicy—though you can kick it up a notch with a teaspoon of cayenne. Paprika, cumin, and cinnamon may decrease the risk of Alzheimer's, and all the spices have an additive effect to decrease cholesterol.

**3 tablespoons** chili powder
**2 tablespoons** paprika
**2 tablespoons** ground cumin
**1 tablespoon** granulated onion
**1 tablespoon** granulated garlic
**1½ teaspoons** crushed red pepper flakes
**2 teaspoons** dried oregano
**1½ teaspoons** freshly ground black pepper
**¼ teaspoon** ground cinnamon
**¼ teaspoon** ground cloves

## POTENTIAL BENEFITS

- High in antioxidants
- Lowers cholesterol
- Strengthens memory

# Daily Power Beverages

**When it comes to getting your spice fix, did you know you can pour it on?** After all, we're already used to adding things to our beverages, but usually they're unhealthy ingredients like sugar or heavy cream. You can take your nutrition to a much, much higher level by swapping in spices for those unnecessary additives. Plus, spicing up your beverages boosts your health sip by sip, while bringing a little mixology fun. I've created these drink recipes for all hours, from morning to late night, but feel free to enjoy them any time!

# Golden Choco-latte

**Serves 1**

(V) (GF)

A robust combination of pure cacao, cinnamon, turmeric, and ginger infused in warm plant-based milk. Mmm . . . doesn't that sound soothing? After a long day, I love to unwind with this drink in the evening. Cacao and the touch of oil help optimize the absorption of turmeric's main antioxidant, curcumin—which can help soothe inflammation—while ginger and cinnamon may help balance your blood sugars while filling your kitchen with a delicious aroma. These are spice combos I can get behind! For extra nutritional credit, be daring—add a tiny pinch of ground black pepper.

**1 cup** non-dairy milk

**⅛ teaspoon** walnut or coconut oil

**¼ teaspoon** ground turmeric*

**¼ teaspoon** ground cinnamon*

**¼ teaspoon** cacao powder*

**⅛ teaspoon** ground ginger*

**Pinch** of freshly ground black pepper (optional)

*Sub spices for: **1 teaspoon** Golden Power Breakfast Blend (page 52)

**1.** In a small saucepan over low heat, combine the milk and oil and let heat until just warm. Add the turmeric, cinnamon, cacao, ginger, and black pepper (if using) and whisk until well combined. Pour into a mug and serve.

# Rachel's Anti-Cancer Power Tonic

**Makes 8 cups**

This tea is one of my signature power beverages—drink it first thing in the morning (or anytime, really!) to naturally detox your system. The turmeric, ginger, and cinnamon are the anti-cancer essentials. The flavor is brightened up with lemon, and my secret tip is to add fennel, dandelion, and parsley to help debloat your belly. Steeping these nourishing ingredients in warm water helps calm your digestive tract and soothe inflammation. I've found that starting my day with this tea really makes all the difference in how I feel! Make a batch and drink it hot or chilled throughout the day.

**2-inch** piece fresh turmeric, peeled and sliced into rounds

**3-inch** piece fresh ginger, peeled and sliced into rounds

**1 teaspoon** ground cinnamon

**½ lemon,** sliced into ½-inch circles

**10 sprigs** fresh parsley and/or fresh mint

**2** dandelion tea bags

**2** fennel tea bags, or 2 teaspoons fennel seeds

**⅛ teaspoon** freshly ground black pepper

**1.** In a medium saucepan over low heat, combine the turmeric, ginger, cinnamon, lemon slices, parsley, mint (if using), dandelion tea bags, fennel tea bags (or seeds, if using), black pepper, and 8 cups water. Bring to a simmer and let cook for 8 to 10 minutes until the spices are fragrant.

**2.** Strain, if desired, and pour into mugs. The tea can also be stored in airtight containers in the fridge for up to 3 days. You can enjoy chilled or reheated before serving.

# Turkish Waker-Upper Coffee

**Serves 2**

It's time to treat yourself. Instead of a typical latte, spice up your daily dose of caffeine with some nutritional perks! Turkish coffee, famous for its strength, is usually made with cardamom. This brew uses espresso and adds some cloves into the mix for an even more deliciously aromatic wake-up call. I enjoy adding a dash of cinnamon on top on my way out the door!

2 **cups** non-dairy milk

1 **teaspoon** ground cinnamon

⅛ **teaspoon** ground cardamom

**Pinch** of ground cloves

2 **shots** espresso

1 **teaspoon** raw or manuka honey (optional)

**1.** In a small saucepan over medium heat, combine the milk, cinnamon, cardamom, and cloves. Bring to a simmer and then immediately remove the saucepan from the heat.

**2.** Add the espresso and honey (if using) to the saucepan and stir until combined. Pour into mugs and serve.

# Matcha 3 Ways

Matcha is having a moment—and for good reason! Matcha is made of powdered green tea leaves and has at least three times the antioxidants of regular green tea. But store-bought matcha lattes are complete sugar-bombs and usually filled with dairy (which may decrease the absorption of matcha's main antioxidant and anticancer compound, EGCG). These three matcha teas use non-dairy milk instead, which adds a nice creaminess while still optimizing nutrient absorption. And spices like cinnamon and turmeric work well with matcha's natural earthiness while delivering even more health benefits. Feel free to add a hint of sweetness—I usually add one juicy date before blending, but you can also use ½ teaspoon maple syrup or coconut nectar.

## Stabilizing Matcha

No more sugar crashes! The combination of ginger, cinnamon, and matcha has been shown to stabilize blood sugar levels and decrease the risk of diabetes.

**Serves 1**

1 **cup** non-dairy milk

¾ **teaspoon** matcha powder

½ **teaspoon** ground cinnamon

⅛ **teaspoon** ground ginger

## Soothing Matcha

This tea features the anti-inflammatory super-star turmeric, which is absorbed even better when combined with a mild oil and a tiny pinch of black pepper (don't worry, you won't taste it!).

**Serves 1**

1 **cup** non-dairy milk

½ **to 1 teaspoon** matcha powder

⅛ **teaspoon** ground turmeric

⅛ **teaspoon** ground ginger

⅛ **teaspoon** avocado oil or walnut oil

**Pinch** of freshly ground black pepper

## Prevention Matcha

Cacao isn't just delicious, it also works with the matcha to boost the cancer-fighting properties of this tea. Drink up!

**Serves 1**

1 **cup** non-dairy milk

¾ **teaspoon** matcha powder

½ **teaspoon** cacao powder

⅛ **teaspoon** ground turmeric

**Pinch** of freshly ground black pepper

**To make each matcha drink,** combine all the ingredients in a blender and pulse for 10 to 15 seconds, until smooth. Transfer the mixture to a small saucepan over medium-low heat. Heat until warmed through to your desired temperature, then pour into a mug and serve. You can also serve these cold by pouring the liquid from the blender into an ice-filled glass.

# Red-Hot Chili Cocoa

**Serves 2**

(v) (GF)

Craving a decadent cup of hot cocoa on a cold winter's day? Throw away those instant hot cocoa packets that are full of unwanted sugars, milk powders, and fillers. Even standard cocoa powder has been stripped of many of chocolate's health benefits. Instead, whip up this power-food version that combines minimally processed cacao with cayenne for a super-powerful cancer-preventive combo. The spicy-sweet combination of flavors is reminiscent of typical Mexican hot chocolate, and it hits the spot during the late afternoon when I need something with a deep, warming flavor. Sometimes I'll even add some ground coffee or a shot of espresso!

**2 cups** non-dairy milk

**3** dried Medjool dates, pitted

**1 tablespoon** cacao powder

**½ teaspoon** ground cinnamon

**⅛ teaspoon** cayenne

**½ teaspoon** ground coffee, or **1 shot** of organic espresso (optional)

**Pinch** of sea salt (optional)

**1.** In a blender, combine the milk, dates, cacao, cinnamon, cayenne, and coffee (if using) and pulse until smooth.

**2.** Pour the mixture into a small saucepan over low heat and bring to a simmer; heat until warmed through to your desired temperature.

**3.** Divide the mixture between two mugs and add a touch of sea salt and stir in, if desired.

# Power Shots

Cheers to your health! These shots are the kind I encourage you to have. Ancient cultures used ginger, vinegar, and spices to boost immune function for thousands of years. While I often take these shots "straight up," you can add a spoonful of grade A maple syrup or raw or manuka honey to help this "medicine" go down.

# Immunity Shot

Bottoms up whenever you think you're coming down with something, or if you're seeking a bit of extra protection during flu season!

**Makes two 2-ounce shots**

½ **cup** coconut water

1 **tablespoon** fresh lemon or orange juice (from about ½ lemon or ¼ orange)

¼ **teaspoon** ground turmeric

¼ **teaspoon** ground ginger

⅛ **teaspoon** freshly ground black pepper

1 **teaspoon** cider vinegar

1 **teaspoon** raw or manuka honey, or maple syrup (optional)

In a tall glass, combine the coconut water, lemon juice, turmeric, ginger, black pepper, cider vinegar, and honey (if using) and whisk until smooth. Divide between two shot glasses and serve. You can keep any extra refrigerated for 2 to 3 days in an airtight container.

# Digestion Booster Shot

Need an extra boost? Whip this up to get your digestive juices going.

**Makes two 2-ounce shots**

¼ **cup** coconut water

2 **tablespoons** freshly squeezed lemon juice (from about 1 lemon)

2 **tablespoons** cider vinegar

⅛ **teaspoon** ground ginger

⅛ **teaspoon** ground cardamom

In a tall glass, combine the coconut water, lemon juice, cider vinegar, ginger, and cardamom, and whisk until smooth. Divide between two shot glasses and serve.

# Metabolism Revving Shot

Cayenne can literally increase the amount of calories your body burns, and the acid in cider vinegar may help burn fat.

**Makes two 2-ounce shots**

¼ **cup** coconut water

2 **tablespoons** freshly squeezed lemon juice (from about 1 lemon)

2 **tablespoons** cider vinegar

⅛ **teaspoon** cayenne

In a tall glass, combine the coconut water, lemon juice, cider vinegar, and cayenne and whisk until smooth. Divide between two shot glasses and serve.

# Saffron and Cardamom Latte

**Serves 1**

(V) (GF)

2 **cups** non-dairy milk

8 **threads** saffron

3 green cardamom pods, crushed with a spoon

⅛ **teaspoon** ground cinnamon

1 **teaspoon** fennel seeds (optional)

Raw or manuka honey, or maple syrup to taste

I make a pot of this healing beverage at least twice a month, and each batch lasts me 3 to 4 days. It's the simplest way I've found to keep saffron as a consistent staple in my diet. This "latte" really helps me jump-start my morning on a high note, thanks to saffron's mood-boosting effects. The soothing saffron and cardamom flavors blend together beautifully, plus they both help strengthen the immune system. And if you're feeling a bit bloated, try adding some fennel seeds to help slim down your tummy!

1. In a small saucepan over medium heat, combine the milk, saffron, cardamom, cinnamon, and fennel seeds (if using), and bring to a boil. Reduce the heat to low and simmer for 8 to 10 minutes until the spices are fragrant.

2. Strain the mixture into a mug and stir in the honey or maple syrup, if desired, and serve.

# Bedtime Recovery Tea

**Serves 2**

(V) (GF)

This tea will soothe aches and pains and get you ready to snooze away! Tart cherry juice has been shown to improve muscle soreness and decrease inflammation, and it's also high in melatonin, which can help improve sleep. The ginger, turmeric, and cinnamon in this tea will fill your home with a relaxing fragrance while adding their own anti-inflammatory effects to the mix. Drink up after a long day, and feel those muscles finally relax!

½ **cup** tart cherry juice

¼ **teaspoon** ground turmeric

¼ **teaspoon** ground ginger

**1 teaspoon** ground cinnamon

**3 to 4** black peppercorns, or a pinch of freshly ground black pepper (optional)

**2** chamomile tea bags

Raw or manuka honey to taste (optional)

**1.** In a small saucepan over medium heat, bring the cherry juice and 2 cups water to a boil.

**2.** Remove the saucepan from the heat and stir in the turmeric, ginger, cinnamon, and peppercorns (if using). Add the tea bags, cover, and steep for 3 to 5 minutes until the tea is a deep reddish brown.

**3.** Remove the tea bags and strain the tea into two mugs. Stir in honey, if desired, and serve.

# Spicy and Sweet Breakfasts

**A spicy morning will perk you up in so many ways.** My patients tell me that getting their spice fix first thing helps them start their day on a high nutritional note, boosting their moods and giving them confidence and motivation throughout the day.

Now, I'm not telling you to pour heaping amounts of cayenne onto your usual breakfast—but if that helps wake you up, go for it! Instead, these recipes let you treat breakfast however you like—hot or cold, on the go or as a long and leisurely affair—while encouraging you to play with both hot and comforting spices to start your day.

# Spiced Zucchini Almond Muffins

**Makes 8 to 10 medium muffins,
or 12 to 16 mini muffins**

(GF)

Here's a hearty grab-and-go breakfast that will keep you full and energized for hours. All four of my kids love them—which is a major feat, given that they question everything I make that contains zucchini! Little do they know that these muffins are loaded with spices to help balance blood sugars and decrease inflammation. You can make the batter into medium muffins for breakfast or into mini muffins for snacks, depending on what kind of muffin tins you have. And you can also easily double this recipe if you want extra muffins on hand.

**1 medium** zucchini, finely grated (about 1 cup)

**2 large** organic eggs

Juice of **1 small** orange (about 3 tablespoons)

**¼ cup** avocado oil or walnut oil

**½ teaspoon** pure vanilla extract

**¼ cup plus 1 tablespoon** raw honey

**2 cups** almond flour

**2 tablespoons** chia seeds

**1 teaspoon** baking soda

**1½ teaspoons** ground cinnamon

**¼ teaspoon** ground nutmeg

**¼ teaspoon** ground allspice

**¼ teaspoon** sea salt

**1.** Preheat the oven to 350°F and line a muffin tin with baking cups.

**2.** In a medium bowl, combine the zucchini, eggs, orange juice, oil, vanilla, and honey and whisk until smooth.

**3.** In a small bowl, combine the almond flour, chia seeds, baking soda, cinnamon, nutmeg, allspice, and salt and stir until well combined Add the flour mixture to the zucchini mixture and gently stir until incorporated and no dry ingredient streaks are remaining.

**4.** Fill the baking cups just over halfway with the batter. Bake for 20 to 25 minutes, until the muffins are brown and fluffy, and a toothpick inserted into the center comes out clean.

**5.** Let the muffins cool a while on a wire rack before serving. Store leftovers in an airtight container in the fridge, where they will keep for 4 to 5 days.

# Power-Spiced Overnight Oats

**Serves 1**

(V) (GF)

For anyone who doesn't have much time in the morning, this one's for you. Rather than cooking the oats on the stovetop, you can simply combine all of the ingredients in a jar, stir it, and throw it in the fridge before crawling into bed. While this recipe is easy to make, it's anything but basic in terms of benefits. By adding a few simple spices, you've easily transformed an unassuming bowl of oatmeal into an antioxidant-rich breakfast. Feel free to get creative—atmeal is the perfect base on which to experiment with your own favorite spices! I like to make a few jars of overnight oats ahead of time so I have several quick grab-and-go breakfasts to use throughout the week. You can either warm up each serving of oats in the morning or eat it chilled.

**½ cup** old-fashioned rolled oats

**1 cup** non-dairy milk

**1 tablespoon** chia seeds

**1 teaspoon** ground cinnamon*

*Sub spices for: **1 teaspoon** Sweet Success Morning Power Blend (page 53) or CinnaPeel Breakfast Blend (page 52), or **1 teaspoon** cacao powder with an optional pinch of cayenne or cinnamon*

**FOR TOPPING (OPTIONAL):**

Nut butter of choice

Berries

Hempseeds or flaxseeds

Cacao nibs

Freshly grated lemon or orange zest

Unsweetened coconut flakes

**1.** In a small jar or container, combine the oats, milk, chia seeds, and cinnamon and stir. Cover and refrigerate overnight.

**2.** Serve chilled or heat the oats gently on the stovetop. Add toppings as desired and serve.

# Butternut Squash and Apple Bake

**Serves 4**

Warm, perfectly sweet bites of apples and butternut squash with cinnamon and spice don't need to be reserved for special occasions. I prescribe this recipe to my stressed-out clients, due to its therapeutic aroma and no-fuss directions (all you need to do is cube, mix, bake, and then take individual portions to go). When the scent of fruit mingled with autumnal spices drifts out of your cubicle, don't blame me if your coworkers stop by to check out your breakfast! When they do, you can tout the antioxidant benefits of ginger and cinnamon and tell them that this combo may help reduce cholesterol levels. But be careful—you may have to share a bite or two! To add a fiber boost, add a tablespoon of chia seeds or ground flaxseed just before serving. The extra fiber will help you feel full longer. You can enjoy this recipe chilled or warm!

**2 large** apples, such as Golden or Fuji, cored and cut into 1- to 2-inch cubes

**1 medium** butternut squash, peeled, seeded, and cubed (about 4 cups)

**2 teaspoons** extra-virgin olive oil or avocado oil

**1 tablespoon** ground cinnamon*

**1 teaspoon** ground allspice*

**½ teaspoon** ground ginger*

Sea salt to taste

**¼ cup** slivered almonds or chopped pecans (optional)

*Sub spices for: **2 teaspoons** Sweet Success Morning Power Blend (page 53)*

**1.** Preheat the oven to 375°F.

**2.** In a medium baking dish, combine the apples, squash, oil, cinnamon, allspice, and ginger, tossing with your hands or a large spoon to ensure everything is evenly coated. Cover with a sheet of parchment paper and a layer of aluminum foil to seal the edges of the baking dish.

**3.** Bake for 45 to 50 minutes, until the squash is tender and can easily be pierced with a fork.

**4.** Remove the dish from the oven and sprinkle with sea salt. Stir before serving and top with nuts, if using.

# Banana Silver Dollar Pancakes

**Makes twenty-four 2-inch pancakes**

These definitely aren't your plain-Jane pancakes! They get a boost of natural sweetness and flavor complexity from ground cinnamon, ginger, and orange peel. These dense cakes (the version with eggs is a bit fluffier than the vegan version) taste great hot or chilled—I love making a big batch of these on the weekend and using the leftovers for an on-the-go snack during the week (it's a favorite among my teen clients). Serve with maple syrup if you like, or, as I often do, some nut butter for some extra protein.

**2 cups** old-fashioned gluten-free rolled oats

**2 cups** non-dairy milk

**2 ripe** medium bananas

**2 large** eggs or Vegan Flax Eggs (see Note)

**2 teaspoons** baking powder

**2 teaspoons** pure vanilla extract

**1 tablespoon** ground cinnamon*

**½ teaspoon** ground ginger*

**1 teaspoon** dried granulated orange peel* (optional)

**2 tablespoons** chia seeds

**1 tablespoon** coconut oil or avocado oil, for greasing

**1 to 2 teaspoons** maple syrup, for serving (optional)

Nut butter, for serving (optional)

*Sub spices for: **1 tablespoon** CinnaPeel Breakfast Blend (page 52)

**1.** In a blender, combine the oats, milk, banana, eggs, baking powder, vanilla, cinnamon, ginger, and orange peel (if using) and pulse until combined. Transfer the batter to a large bowl and stir in the chia seeds.

**2.** Heat the oil in a medium skillet over medium heat. When the oil is shimmering, use a large spoon to scoop the batter from the bowl and pour it into the skillet to create 2-inch rounds. Cook for 1 to 2 minutes, until the underside of each pancake is light golden brown. Flip the pancakes and cook for 1 to 2 minutes more, until the other side is golden brown.

**3.** Transfer the pancakes to a large plate and repeat the above steps for the remaining batter. Serve the pancakes with maple syrup or nut butter, if desired.

---

**NOTE** *To make 1 Vegan Flax Egg, mix 1 tablespoon ground flaxseeds with 2½ tablespoons water. Let rest for 5 minutes to thicken before using. (Don't forget to make two of these for this recipe!)*

# Cinnamon-Quinoa Granola

**Makes 3 cups**

Granola gets a bad rep in the nutrition world because store-bought versions are loaded with added sugars that are not helpful for your waistline or your health. This granola is the opposite—it's low-calorie, low-sugar (you can even omit the maple syrup completely if you want to make it sugar-free), and loaded with protein, fiber, and omega-3 fats. But what really takes it to the next level is the combination of heart-healthy, anti-inflammatory, and blood-sugar-stabilizing spices. So don't be afraid to indulge in this granola whenever you need a sweet, crunchy snack! My favorite way to enjoy it is with a tablespoon of chia seeds and a few splashes of non-dairy milk.

**4 cups** cooked quinoa

**¼ cup** hempseeds

**½ cup** unsweetened coconut flakes

**2 tablespoons** ground cinnamon*

**½ teaspoon** ground ginger*

**1 teaspoon** granulated orange peel*

**1 to 2 tablespoons** maple syrup (optional)

*Sub spices for: **2 tablespoons** CinnaPeel Breakfast Blend (page 52)*

**1.** Preheat the oven to 375°F and line a rimmed baking sheet with parchment paper.

**2.** Combine the quinoa, hempseeds, coconut flakes, cinnamon, ginger, orange peel, and maple syrup (if using) and toss until everything is thoroughly coated.

**3.** Spread the mixture evenly in a single layer on the prepared baking sheet. Bake for 20 to 25 minutes, stirring once halfway through, until the granola is golden and fragrant. Let cool.

**4.** Serve or store in an airtight container (refrigerated or at room temperature) for up to 2 weeks.

# Spiced Sweet Potato Pockets

**Serves 4**

(V) (GF)

Don't settle for a plain old sweet potato when you can enjoy these hot pockets of creamy, spicy goodness—sweet potatoes infused with a warming blend of anti-inflammatory spices, protein-rich nut butter, and chia seeds for a hit of fiber. This balanced breakfast will keep you satisfied for hours. I like to roast a few sweet potatoes at a time so I have several breakfasts and snacks that I can quickly use throughout the week.

**4 medium** sweet potatoes, scrubbed

**¼ cup** chia seeds

**2 teaspoons** ground cinnamon

**½ teaspoon** ground nutmeg, ginger, turmeric, allspice, or cloves

**2 tablespoons** nut butter

Tahini for serving (optional)

**1.** Preheat the oven to 400°F and line a rimmed baking sheet with parchment paper.

**2.** Place the sweet potatoes on the prepared baking sheet and bake for 45 minutes to 1 hour until tender and easily pierced with a fork. Remove the baking sheet from the oven and allow the potatoes to cool for 5 to 10 minutes.

**3.** Split each potato open lengthwise with a knife. Divide the chia seeds and spices among the potatoes and use a fork to mash the ingredients into the flesh. Drizzle each potato with nut butter and tahini (if using). Serve warm or let cool to room temperature if you're taking the potatoes on the go.

**NOTE** *For a myriad of nut-butter and spice mix-ins, see page 48.*

# Fiesta Scramble

**Serves 4**

(V) (GF)

This is my favorite savory breakfast: it comes together in 5 minutes, it's high in protein, and it keeps me fueled for hours. It's ridiculously flexible, too. You can throw in whatever vegetables are in your fridge—raw spinach, leftover roasted Brussels sprouts, fresh cherry tomatoes, broccoli, you name it! Here I use tofu for the scramble, but you can sub eggs if you prefer. The nonnegotiable ingredients are turmeric, garlic, and black pepper. This combination works to reduce the risk of cardiovascular disease and promotes blood vessel health. Plus, it just tastes *good*!

**1 tablespoon** extra-virgin olive oil

**1 medium** yellow onion, chopped (about 2 cups)

**2** garlic cloves, minced

**2** red bell peppers, seeded and chopped

**2 (14- to 16-ounce)** packages firm tofu, drained, or **6 large** organic eggs, lightly beaten

**1 teaspoon** chili powder*

**½ teaspoon** ground cumin*

**½ teaspoon** ground turmeric*

**¼ teaspoon** granulated garlic*

**¼ teaspoon** freshly ground black pepper

**Pinch** of cayenne or crushed red pepper flakes

**2 tablespoons** nutritional yeast (optional)

**2 cups** store-bought tomato sauce (optional; for tofu scramble only)

**2 cups** cooked black beans, rinsed and drained (see page 45)

Sea salt to taste

**1** avocado, sliced, for serving (optional)

Salsa, for serving (optional)

*Sub spices for: **2 teaspoons** Everything Savory Power Blend (page 52)*

1.  Heat the oil in a medium skillet over medium-high heat. When the oil is shimmering, add the onion, minced garlic, and bell peppers and cook, stirring occasionally, for 3 to 4 minutes, until the onion is translucent.

2.  Add the tofu, chili powder, cumin, turmeric, granulated garlic, black pepper, cayenne, and nutritional yeast (if using) to the skillet. Break the tofu apart with a wooden spoon until it resembles scrambled eggs and appears chunky. Stir in the tomato sauce. (If you're using eggs, use a rubber spatula to stir the mixture, about 2 minutes, until the eggs are just cooked through; omit the tomato sauce.)

3.  Stir the black beans into the skillet and cook for 2 to 3 minutes more until beans are warmed. Season with salt to taste and divide the scramble among plates. Serve with avocado slices and salsa, if desired.

# Apple-Zested Muesli

**Makes 3 cups**

(V) (GF)

When life gets busy (as it sometimes does with my four children!), it's occasionally best to strip breakfast down to the basics. This muesli—a type of Swiss granola made without oil and added sweeteners—is a simple yet nourishing breakfast. You can taste each ingredient and enjoy the flavors of sweet dried apple, rich vanilla, and warming cinnamon in every bowl. If you have fresh lemons, sprinkle some grated zest into the mix—not only will it brighten up the muesli, but you'll get a fresh boost of its unique cancer-fighting compounds. I love sprinkling this muesli on top of smoothies, using it as a cereal with non-dairy milk, stirring it into probiotic-packed yogurt, and, of course, snacking on it straight out of the oven!

4 apples, such as Golden or Fuji, cored and diced

**1 cup** old-fashioned rolled oats

¼ **cup** chia seeds

**1 tablespoon plus 1 teaspoon** ground cinnamon*

½ **teaspoon** pure vanilla extract

**1 tablespoon** freshly grated lemon zest (optional)

*Sub spices for: **1 tablespoon plus 1 teaspoon** Sweet Success Morning Power Blend (page 53), or **1 tablespoon plus 1 teaspoon** Cinna-Peel Breakfast Blend (page 52)*

**1.**   Preheat the oven to 425°F and line a rimmed baking sheet with parchment paper.

**2.**   In a large bowl, combine the apples, oats, chia seeds, cinnamon, vanilla, and lemon zest (if using) and, using your hands, toss until the apples are fully coated. Spread the mixture evenly in a single layer on the prepared baking sheet.

**3.**   Bake for 30 to 40 minutes, until the muesli is golden brown. Let cool for 5 minutes before serving.

**4.**   This muesli can also be refrigerated and stored in an airtight container, such as a mason jar, for up to 10 days.

# Savory Sorghum Porridge

**Serves 2**

 V GF

Porridge doesn't always have to be sweet! This fragrant bowl—almost like breakfast risotto—is packed with immune-boosting ingredients. Sorghum, mushrooms, garlic, onions, chia, and flax all promote gut health and a strong immune system. Rosemary, turmeric, and black pepper work synergistically as well. This porridge with all its incredible ingredients makes a great start to a healthy morning, but I've even eaten this for lunch and dinner, too! If you don't have sorghum on hand, you can substitute rolled oats or quinoa.

**1 teaspoon** extra-virgin olive oil

**¼ medium** yellow onion, sliced (about ½ cup)

**1** garlic clove, minced

**⅛ teaspoon** ground turmeric

**¼ teaspoon** paprika

**Pinch** of dried rosemary

**⅛ teaspoon** freshly ground black pepper

**1 cup** thinly sliced cremini mushrooms

**½ medium** red bell pepper, seeded and diced

**1 cup** gluten-free sorghum, cooked according to package directions

**1 tablespoon** chia seeds, or **2 tablespoons** ground flaxseed

**1 teaspoon** nutritional yeast (optional)

Sea salt to taste

1.  Heat the oil in a medium skillet over medium heat. When the oil is shimmering, add the onion and garlic and cook for 3 to 5 minutes, until the onion is softened.

2.  Add the turmeric, paprika, rosemary, and black pepper to the skillet, stir, and cook for 30 seconds to allow the spices to bloom. When the mixture is fragrant, add the mushrooms and bell pepper to the skillet and sauté for 3 to 5 minutes more, until just tender.

3.  Stir in the cooked sorghum, chia seeds or flaxseed, and nutritional yeast (if using) and season with salt.

4.  Divide the mixture between two bowls and serve.

# Chickpea Shakshuka

**Serves 4**

(VO) (GF)

Shakshuka has long been a popular dish in areas such as North Africa and Israel, but it has recently become a popular member of breakfast rotations in the States as well! Here is a flavorful and easy vegan twist that combines chickpeas in a spicy tomato sauce with paprika, cumin, cayenne, and fresh parsley. Paprika and cayenne deliver a double dose of the potent antioxidant capsaicin, and the flavors of this dynamic duo really shine in the tomato sauce. You can enjoy shakshuka any time of the day; for lunch or dinner, serve it alongside a salad or roasted vegetables. You can also use organic eggs in place of the chickpeas, if you prefer.

**1 tablespoon** extra-virgin olive oil or avocado oil

**1 medium** yellow onion, chopped (about 2 cups)

**1 teaspoon** paprika

**¾ teaspoon** ground cumin

**¼ teaspoon** cayenne

**⅛ teaspoon** freshly ground black pepper

**2** garlic cloves, minced

**1 medium** bell pepper (any color), seeded and chopped

**7** ripe Roma tomatoes, diced (about 6 cups), or **1 (28-ounce)** can diced tomatoes

**¾ cup** store-bought tomato sauce

**2 cups** cooked chickpeas, rinsed and drained (see page 45), or **4 large** organic eggs

Sea salt to taste

**¼ cup** chopped fresh parsley, for garnish

**Pinch** of crushed red pepper flakes, for garnish

**1.** Heat the oil in a large cast-iron skillet over medium heat. When the oil is shimmering, add the onion and cook for 2 to 3 minutes, until the onion begins to soften. Add the paprika, cumin, cayenne, and black pepper and continue cooking for 30 seconds more.

**2.** When the spices are fragrant, add the garlic and bell pepper and cook for 2 minutes more. Stir in the tomatoes and tomato sauce, cover, and reduce the heat to medium-low. Cook for about 5 minutes more, until everything is well combined and the tomato sauce has started to reduce.

**3.** Stir in the chickpeas; or, if you're using eggs, make four indentations in the tomato mixture and crack an egg into each one. Reduce the heat to low, cover the skillet again, and continue to simmer for 8 to 10 minutes, until all the ingredients and spices seem fragrant and well-integrated (or until the egg yolks are set but still slightly runny). Season with salt and top with parsley and red pepper flakes.

**4.** Divide the shakshuka among four plates and serve.

# Israeli Breakfast Sampler

**Serves 2**

One of my favorite things about visiting Israel is enjoying an Israeli-style breakfast. The local tradition of sharing a spread of herby cucumber-tomato salad, bowls of hummus, spiced olives, and eggs has made for some wonderful memories. Back at home, we make it as a balanced meal that fuels us for a day of activities! I love that this sampler packs in at least 2 cups of produce (and plenty of protein) before noon. Here I've used some of my favorite components of an Israeli breakfast, with a spiced-up twist: Sumac, parsley, and lemon juice not only hit your taste buds with a fresh, tangy flavor in the morning, but they also exert powerful antioxidant effects.

## FOR THE SALAD

**4** Persian cucumbers, diced

**4** ripe Roma tomatoes, diced

**½ cup** chopped fresh parsley

**½ teaspoon** ground sumac

**1½ tablespoons** extra-virgin olive oil

**1½ tablespoons** freshly squeezed lemon juice (from about 1 lemon)

Sea salt to taste

## FOR THE SIDE DISHES (OPTIONAL)

**2** sunny-side up or hard-boiled organic eggs (sliced in half), sprinkled with paprika, coarse black pepper, and crushed red pepper flakes

Spiced-Up Crispy Chickpeas (page 125)

Green olives

Hummus 3 Ways (or More!) (page 138) with paprika and ground sumac

Tahini with chopped fresh parsley and za'atar

**1.** Prepare the salad: In a medium bowl, combine the cucumbers, tomatoes, parsley, sumac, oil, and lemon juice and toss well. Season with salt.

**2.** Serve the salad with the sides of your choice.

---

**TIP** *Add a sumac shaker on your kitchen table. I add it to everything—salads, vegetables, grains, and protein!*

# Tzimmes Oat Crumble

**Serves 8**

(V) (GF)

Who eats carrots for breakfast? I do! Tzimmes is a sweet Jewish stew that is traditionally eaten for the New Year, celebrating the start of a sweet year ahead. This tzimmes recipe is based on my mother's recipe, which is heavily spiced with cinnamon, and every time I make it, the sweet scent of cinnamon brings back warm and fuzzy childhood memories. I added oats to this classic dish to create a year-round breakfast dish that everyone can love. Although impossible to pronounce, tzimmes ('tsi-mes) is naturally sweet on the tongue and makes a great family-favorite fall and winter side dish. Top your serving with 1 tablespoon of chia seeds for a fiber boost, if you like.

**14 medium** carrots, sliced into ¼-inch rounds (about 8 cups)

**2 dozen** dried prunes (sulfur-free, no-sugar-added varieties), pitted and cut in half

**2 tablespoons** ground cinnamon

**2 tablespoons** coconut oil, walnut oil, or vegan butter

**1 tablespoon** almond flour

**1 cup** old-fashioned rolled oats

**2 tablespoons** freshly squeezed lemon juice (from about 1 lemon)

**1 to 2 tablespoons** maple syrup or raw or manuka honey (optional)

**1.** Preheat the oven to 300°F.

**2.** Place the carrots in a large, heavy-bottomed, ovenproof saucepan (such as a Dutch oven), cover them with water by at least 1 inch, and bring to a boil over high heat. Reduce the heat to medium-low, cover, and simmer for 30 minutes until the carrots are tender.

**3.** Add the prunes, cinnamon, and oil to the saucepan and continue to simmer uncovered for 1 hour.

**4.** Add the almond flour and oats and stir to incorporate. Transfer to the oven and bake uncovered for about 1 hour, until the liquid is cooked down and has formed a glaze on the carrots.

**5.** Drizzle the tzimmes with lemon juice and honey (if using) and serve warm or chilled.

**6.** You can store the tzimmes in an airtight container in the fridge for up to 4 days.

# Mains That Pack a Punch

**I purposely made these recipes simple, because eating healthy shouldn't be a hassle—complicated recipes scare people out of the kitchen!** I let the spices do the heavy lifting for you so that you don't need to be a three-star chef to make delicious meals—but you'll be spicing like one.

You'll notice that I emphasize vegetables and plant-based proteins, because that's how I eat and what I recommend to my patients, but of course you'll also find some meat and fish options if that's what you're looking for. All in all, these recipes are clean and pure dishes that steer clear of the stuff you don't need, namely processed sugars and refined grains. No matter what your tastes are, and whether it's lunch or dinner inspiration you're seeking, you'll find something that appeals to you. Bon appétit!

# Lentil Salad
## with Spicy Vinaigrette

**Serves 4 or 5**

(V) (GF)

This recipe is one of my staple dishes: I make a big batch on Sunday night and use it for family lunches throughout the week. Not only do cumin and coriander work synergistically to deliver antioxidant and antimicrobial benefits, but lentils are also ridiculously filling (thanks to the fiber and protein boost). I choose petite lentils because of their extra-firm texture and slightly spicy flavor that blends beautifully with this piquant vinaigrette. This lentil salad is equally delicious on top of a bed of greens with some sliced bell pepper and grape tomatoes as it is by itself, or alongside the Ruby Red Beet Salad (page 120).

**2 cups** dried petite black or green lentils

**¾ cup** chopped fresh parsley

**3 tablespoons** extra-virgin olive oil

**2 tablespoons** red wine vinegar

**2 tablespoons** freshly squeezed lemon juice (from about 1 lemon)

**¼ teaspoon** granulated garlic

**½ teaspoon** ground cumin

**¼ teaspoon** cayenne

**⅛ teaspoon** freshly ground black pepper

**⅛ teaspoon** ground coriander (optional)

**⅛ teaspoon** ground fenugreek (optional)

Sea salt to taste

**1.**  In a medium saucepan over medium-high heat, bring 5 cups water to a boil. Add the lentils, reduce the heat to medium-low, and cook for 25 to 30 minutes, until the lentils are tender but not overcooked. Drain the lentils in a colander and rinse with cold water until slightly cooled.

**2.**  In a medium bowl, combine the lentils, parsley, oil, vinegar, lemon juice, garlic, cumin, cayenne, black pepper, coriander and fenugreek (if using), and salt and stir until combined. Season to taste with additional salt, cover, and chill for 1 to 2 hours before serving.

# Simple Weeknight Salmon
## with Chimichurri

**Serves 4**

Intimidated by fish? Don't be! I make this dish twice a week for my husband and kids, because it takes just 10 minutes to prepare, and there's no messy cleanup! Plus, it makes tasty and lean leftovers for lunch the next day. Turmeric's anti-inflammatory benefits are maximized when combined with the omega-3 fats found in fish. I enjoy pairing this dish with the Za'atar-Roasted Cauliflower (page 118) to create a light yet hearty meal.

**4** wild salmon fillets (5 to 6 ounces each)

**2 teaspoons** extra-virgin olive oil

**½ teaspoon** paprika*

**¼ teaspoon** granulated garlic*

**¼ teaspoon** ground turmeric*

**⅛ teaspoon** ground cumin*

**⅛ teaspoon** freshly ground black pepper*

Sea salt to taste

Juice of **1 to 2** lemons

**¼ cup** Chimichurri Sauce (page 134)

*Sub spices for: **¾ teaspoon** Everything Savory Power Blend (page 52) plus **½ teaspoon** Veggie Power-Up Blend (page 52)*

**1.** Preheat the broiler and line a rimmed baking sheet with parchment paper.

**2.** Place the fish, skin side down, on the baking sheet and use your fingertips to rub each fillet with olive oil. Season the fillets evenly with the paprika, garlic, turmeric, cumin, black pepper, and a sprinkle of sea salt.

**3.** Broil for 5 to 7 minutes, until the salmon is cooked through and flakes easily when pricked with a fork.

**4.** Divide the salmon among plates, drizzle each with lemon juice and the chimichurri, and serve.

# Black Bean Choco Chili

**Serves 6**

(V) (GF)

Chocolate and chiles are a flavorful combination featured in Oaxacan mole sauce. Preparing traditional mole is a complicated, all-day affair, which is where this quick and easy chocolate-chili dish comes in! It captures the rich and savory flavors of mole but is a breeze to make any day of the week. Cumin, paprika, and chili powder will warm you from the inside out, while the cacao delivers delectable depth and even more nutritional perks. This chili pairs well with quinoa and roasted vegetables as a side.

**1 tablespoon** extra-virgin olive oil or avocado oil

**1 medium** yellow onion, chopped (about 2 cups)

**3 garlic cloves**, minced

**1 jalapeño pepper**, seeded and chopped

**1½ tablespoons** chili powder

**1½ teaspoons** ground cumin

**2 teaspoons** cacao powder

**⅛ teaspoon** freshly ground black pepper

**1 medium** sweet potato, peeled and cubed (about 2 cups)

**3 cups** cooked black beans, rinsed and drained (see page 45)

**1 (28-ounce)** can crushed tomatoes (about 3 cups)

**3 cups** low-sodium chicken or vegetable broth

Sea salt to taste

**1.**  Heat the oil in a large saucepan over medium-high heat. When the oil is shimmering, add the onion and cook for 2 to 3 minutes, until the onion is translucent. Add the garlic and jalapeño and continue to cook for 2 minutes more. Add the chili powder, cumin, cacao, and black pepper and stir for about 30 seconds, or until well combined.

**2.**  Add the sweet potato, black beans, tomatoes, and broth and over medium-high heat bring to a boil. Reduce the heat to low and simmer for 45 minutes to 1 hour, until the chili has thickened considerably. Season with salt and serve.

# Glowing Green Frittata

**Serves 4**

(GF)

Frittatas don't have to be just for breakfast, although this makes for great brunch leftovers. Inspired by the Persian dish kuku, this frittata is packed with herbs. It is rich in cancer-fighting beta-carotene (basil, paprika, and cayenne) and the anti-inflammatory duo of turmeric and black pepper. You can add any vegetables you like—zucchini, mushrooms, and spinach are my favorites. You can make this dish without the beans. Serving the frittata with a drizzle of tahini works magic as well.

**2 tablespoons** extra-virgin olive oil, plus more for greasing

**3 cups** chopped fresh parsley

**1½ cups** chopped fresh cilantro

**¼ cup** chopped fresh basil or dill

**3** scallions (white and green parts), coarsely chopped

**1½ teaspoons** baking powder

**2 teaspoons** ground turmeric*

**¾ teaspoon** granulated garlic*

**½ teaspoon** freshly ground black pepper

**1 teaspoon** crushed red pepper flakes

**¼ teaspoon** sea salt

**6 large** organic eggs

**2 cups** cooked lentils or cooked white beans, drained and rinsed (optional; see page 45)

*\* Sub spices for: **2 teaspoons** Veggie Power-Up Blend (page 52)*

1. Preheat the oven to 375°F and lightly brush the bottom and sides of an 8 × 8-inch baking dish or 9-inch round cake pan with olive oil.

2. In a food processor, combine the parsley, cilantro, basil, scallions, and 2 tablespoons of the oil and pulse for 30 to 40 seconds, until the mixture resembles a coarse paste. Set aside.

3. In a large bowl, whisk the baking powder, turmeric, garlic, black pepper, red pepper flakes, and salt. Add 1 egg and whisk until well combined, then add the remaining eggs and whisk until just combined.

4. Gently fold the herb mixture into the egg mixture and stir in the lentils, if using. Pour the mixture into the prepared pan and smooth the top with a spoon.

5. Bake for about 25 minutes, or until the center of the frittata is firm and has risen slightly (it will fall once you remove it from the oven and set it aside to cool). Cover the frittata with a moist towel to steam it and let cool for 10 minutes with the towel on. Cut into squares or triangles and serve.

6. Store leftovers in a sealed container and refrigerate for 3 to 4 days. You can rewarm or serve at room temperature.

# Moroccan Chicken Stew

**Serves 4 to 6**

(VO) (GF)

This dish was inspired by my daughter Alexia, who requested a flavorful chicken dish for her school lunches. The cumin and coriander boost each other's antioxidant activities; garlic, ginger, and cayenne work together to decrease cholesterol. For a vegan option, you can substitute 3 cups cooked chickpeas for the chicken.

**2 medium** yellow onions, sliced (about 4 cups)

**8 to 10 medium** Roma tomatoes, quartered

**4** garlic cloves, chopped

**1 heaping tablespoon** peeled and chopped fresh ginger

**2 tablespoons** extra-virgin olive oil

**4** boneless, skinless, organic free-range chicken breasts, or **3 cups** (cooked) chickpeas

Salt and freshly ground black pepper

**1 tablespoon** ground cumin*

**1 teaspoon** ground turmeric*

**2 teaspoons** ground coriander*

**2 teaspoons** ground cinnamon*

**⅛ teaspoon** cayenne*

**2 medium** carrots, sliced into ¼ inch rounds

**2 cups** low-sodium chicken or vegetable broth

**1 tablespoon** red wine vinegar

**5** dried Medjool dates, pitted and diced

Cooked quinoa, for serving

*Sub spices for: **2 ½ tablespoons** Moroccan Roll Blend (page 53)

1. In a food processor, combine half of the onion with the tomatoes, garlic, and ginger and pulse for 1 minute, until it resembles a salsa. Set aside.

2. Heat 1 tablespoon of the oil in a medium skillet over medium heat. Season both sides of the chicken breasts with salt and pepper. When the oil is shimmering, add the chicken breasts and cook for 2 minutes on each side, until browned but not fully cooked through. Transfer the chicken to a plate.

3. Add the remaining 1 tablespoon of oil to the skillet and increase the heat to medium-high. Add the remaining onion and cook for 5 to 6 minutes, stirring frequently, until lightly browned and softened. Add the cumin, turmeric, coriander, cinnamon, cayenne, and a pinch of black pepper and cook, stirring to combine, for 1 minute until the spices are very fragrant.

4. Add the tomato mixture, chicken (or chickpeas, if using), carrots, broth, and vinegar to the skillet and reduce the heat to a simmer. Cover and cook for 25 to 30 minutes more, or until the chicken is tender and fully cooked through. Season to taste with salt.

5. Remove the chicken from the skillet and transfer it to a plate. Use forks to shred the chicken into bite-size pieces. Add the chicken back into the skillet and stir in the dates. Serve at once, alongside cooked quinoa.

# Anti-inflammatory Chickpea Curry

**Serves 4**

(V) (GF)

Curries are outstanding examples of traditional spicing. I think of them as medicinal stews because they're packed with some of the world's most potent spices: ginger, turmeric, cumin, and black pepper! The hearty chopped vegetables are full of fiber and give this curry a satisfyingly chunky texture. Serve this over steamed quinoa or brown rice.

**1 tablespoon** olive oil, walnut oil, or avocado oil

**1 medium** yellow onion, chopped (about 2 cups)

**1 teaspoon** peeled and minced fresh ginger

**1½ tablespoons** curry powder

**½ teaspoon** ground cumin

**¼ teaspoon** ground turmeric

**2 medium** carrots, cut into ¼-inch rounds (about 2 cups)

**1 medium** cauliflower head, chopped into florets (about 4 cups)

**1 cup** green beans, cut into 2-inch pieces

**1 medium** red or orange bell pepper, seeded and sliced

**3 cups** cooked chickpeas, rinsed and drained (see page 45)

**1 cup** unsweetened coconut milk

Sea salt and freshly ground black pepper to taste

**1.** Heat the oil in a large skillet over medium heat. When the oil is shimmering, add the onion and ginger and cook for 3 to 5 minutes, until the onion is softened. Add the curry powder, cumin, and turmeric and cook for about 30 seconds, or until the spices are fragrant.

**2.** Stir in the carrots, cauliflower, green beans, and bell pepper and cook for 5 to 7 minutes more until the vegetables and spices are well combined. Reduce the heat to low, add the chickpeas, and cover. Cook 5 to 7 minutes more, until the vegetables are tender but not mushy.

**3.** Remove the skillet from the heat. Add the coconut milk and stir until incorporated. Season with salt and pepper to taste and serve.

# Vegan Creamy Brussels Sprout Caesar

**Serves 4**

Brussels sprouts replace romaine here for a top-of-the-line, cancer-fighting vegetable side dish with a potent infusion of anti-inflammatory spices in the dressing. The result is a light yet indulgent salad that won't get soggy like traditional Caesar salad does, so you can make it for dinner and have leftovers with the same level of crunch the next day. You can serve this salad topped with your protein of choice—my go-tos are chickpeas or Spiced Crispy Tofu (page 110).

**1½ tablespoons** avocado oil or extra-virgin olive oil

**2 pounds** Brussels sprouts, cores removed and thinly sliced (about 6 cups)

**¼ teaspoon** granulated garlic*

**¼ teaspoon** granulated onion*

**¼ teaspoon** ground turmeric*

**½ teaspoon** dried parsley*

**Pinch** of sea salt

**⅛ teaspoon** freshly ground black pepper

Crushed red pepper flakes to taste

**¼ cup plus 2 tablespoons** Vegan Caesar Dressing (page 136)

**1 cup** raw sunflower seeds or pumpkin seeds

*Sub spices for: **1 teaspoon** Veggie Power-Up Blend (page 52)*

**1.** Heat the oil in a large skillet over medium-high heat. When the oil is shimmering, add the Brussels sprouts and cook, stirring frequently, for 4 to 5 minutes, or until they are just beginning to wilt. Reduce the heat to medium-low and cook for 3 minutes more.

**2.** Add the garlic, onion, turmeric, parsley, salt, black pepper, and red pepper flakes and stir until the Brussels sprouts are evenly coated.

**3.** Transfer the Brussels sprouts to a large bowl, add the dressing and the sunflower seeds, and toss to combine. Serve warm or chilled. Leftovers can be stored in the refrigerator in an airtight container for up to 2 days.

# Baked Falafel

## with Green Goddess Fenugreek Tahini Sauce

**Serves 4**

Ⓥ ⒢Ⓕ

Falafel is one of my favorite foods, but I don't always want to eat it deep-fried. Fortunately, this baked version still satisfies my falafel craving, and the tofu and quinoa not only boost the protein content of this dish but also keep the falafel extra moist. You can swap chickpeas for cooked lentils if you prefer. The anti-inflammatory spices really shine (both in terms of flavor and nutrition) when combined with the fenugreek sauce, which works with the garlic and turmeric in the falafel to lower cholesterol and maintain cardiovascular health. Mmm . . . this recipe satisfies both my heart and my stomach!

**1½ cups** cooked quinoa

**2 cups** cooked chickpeas, rinsed and drained

**½ cup** chopped fresh cilantro

**½ teaspoon** granulated garlic*

**1 teaspoon** ground cumin*

**1 teaspoon** paprika*

**¾ teaspoon** ground turmeric*

**¼ teaspoon** cayenne

**¼ teaspoon** freshly ground black pepper

**½ teaspoon** sea salt

**6 to 7 ounces** firm organic tofu

**1½ tablespoons** extra-virgin olive oil

Green Goddess Fenugreek Tahini Sauce (page 131), for serving

*Sub spices for: **2 teaspoons** Everything Savory Power Blend (page 52)*

**1.** Preheat the oven to 400°F and line a rimmed baking sheet with parchment paper.

**2.** In a food processor, combine the quinoa, chickpeas, cilantro, garlic, cumin, paprika, turmeric, cayenne, black pepper, and sea salt and pulse for about 30 seconds, until the ingredients appear well incorporated yet still grainy. Transfer the falafel mixture to a large bowl and set it aside.

**3.** Combine the block of tofu (you can break it up into pieces with your hands if you desire) and oil in the same food processor (no need to clean it first) and pulse for about 10 seconds, or until smooth. Add the tofu to the falafel mixture and stir with a spoon until well combined.

**4.** Using your hands, form the falafel mixture into 24 1-inch ping-pong-size balls. Space the falafel ½ inch apart on the prepared baking sheet and bake for about 25 minutes, or until golden brown.

**5.** Transfer the falafel to a serving plate and drizzle with the Green Goddess Fenugreek Tahini Sauce.

# Spiced Crispy Tofu

**Serves 3 or 4**

(V) (GF)

Tofu shouldn't be left to vegan and Chinese restaurants. It's a high-protein, versatile base that can take on basically any flavor profile you can dream up! This recipe is super easy—in just 15 minutes you get a deliciously diverse, crispy protein. Make it once and you'll master the recipe, giving you the flexibility to change up your spice game. Serve these crispy bites of tofu on top of greens or roasted veggies along with brown rice or Immune Support Yellow Quinoa with Parsley and Almonds (page 126). Tofu pairs well with just about anything, so feel free to get creative with your own favorite spice blends!

**1 (16-ounce)** package extra-firm organic sprouted tofu, drained, patted dry, and cubed

**1 tablespoon** extra-virgin olive or avocado oil

Pinch of sea salt

**SEASONING OPTIONS (CHOOSE ONE OF THE FOLLOWING)**

**1½ teaspoons** curry powder

**1½ teaspoons** Chinese five-spice plus **¼ teaspoon** cayenne (optional: drizzle with **1 tablespoon** low-sodium tamari sauce after you pull it out of the oven)

**2 teaspoons** Everything Savory Power Blend (page 52)

**1.** Preheat the oven to 375°F and line a rimmed baking sheet with parchment paper.

**2.** In a medium bowl, combine the tofu, oil, salt, and seasoning of choice, gently stirring to coat the tofu thoroughly. Spread the tofu evenly in a single layer on the prepared baking sheet and bake for 12 to 15 minutes, until crispy and golden brown. Serve immediately.

# Tex-Mex Wraps

**Serves 4**

(VO) (GF)

Taco Tuesday just got a facelift! Store-bought taco spice mixes are often heavy on salt and polluted with sugar, fillers, and other chemicals. These tacos instead rely on potent amounts of the spices traditionally used in tacos, so you can reap major antioxidant and anti-inflammatory benefits. Use quinoa as the main component to truly let the spices shine through, or make the beef version, if you desire. My favorite way to enjoy these tacos is in lettuce cups with a scoop of fresh salsa, cubed avocado, fresh cilantro, and a splash of fresh lime juice. Or, if you prefer a traditional wrapping for your taco, feel free to use organic corn tortillas instead of lettuce.

**1 tablespoon** avocado oil or extra-virgin olive oil

**1 medium** yellow onion, diced (about 2 cups)

**3** garlic cloves, minced

**½ teaspoon** ground cumin*

**½ teaspoon** paprika*

**1 teaspoon** chili powder*

**¼ teaspoon** granulated garlic*

**¼ teaspoon** cayenne*

**⅛ teaspoon** freshly ground black pepper

**3 cups** cooked quinoa or 1 pound grass-fed ground beef

**Pinch** of sea salt

**8** red-leaf lettuce leaves (or any lettuce of choice) or organic corn tortillas

*Sub spices for: **2 teaspoons** Tex-Mex Power Blend (page 53) plus optional **½ teaspoon** crushed red pepper flakes for additional heat*

### FOR TOPPINGS (OPTIONAL)

**½ cup** homemade salsa or your favorite store-bought variety

**1** avocado, chopped

**1 tablespoon** nutritional yeast

**1** lime, cut into wedges

**1.** Heat the oil in a medium skillet over medium heat. When the oil is shimmering, add the onions and minced garlic and cook for 3 to 5 minutes, until the onion is softened.

**2.** Add the cumin, paprika, chili powder, granulated garlic, cayenne, and black pepper and cook for 30 seconds, stirring occasionally, until the spices are fragrant.

**3.** Add the quinoa and stir until well incorporated (or, if using beef, add and stir frequently to prevent clumping, until browned and cooked through). Season with salt and remove from the heat.

**4.** Scoop about ¼ cup of the filling into each lettuce leaf and serve with the desired toppings.

# Immunity Turmeric Soup

**Makes 12 cups**

Ⓥ ⒼⒻ

Whenever anyone in my family is feeling under the weather, I whip up a pot of this soup. With heavy doses of turmeric, ginger, and garlic, it's ridiculously healing and anti-inflammatory; you can add some cayenne pepper for a slight kick that can help clear sinuses! Even if you're not sick, I recommend drinking a bean-less variation of this soup a couple times per week throughout the flu season—heck, I drink it year-round!

**1 tablespoon** extra-virgin olive oil

**1 medium** onion, chopped (about 2 cups)

**3** garlic cloves, minced

**1 medium** carrot, sliced into ¼-inch rounds (about 1 cup)

**2** celery stalks, chopped

**1 tablespoon** ground turmeric

**½ teaspoon** ground ginger

**¼ teaspoon** freshly ground black pepper

**¼ teaspoon** cayenne

**8 cups** low-sodium vegetable broth

**1 medium** cauliflower head, cored and cut into florets (about 4 cups)

**2 medium** zucchini, diced (3 to 4 cups)

**4 cups** chopped kale or Swiss chard (9-10 ounces)

**2 cups** cooked cannellini beans, rinsed and drained (see page 45)

1. Heat the oil in a large saucepan over medium heat. When the oil is shimmering, add the onion and cook for 3 to 4 minutes, until softened. Add the garlic and cook 1 minute more.

2. Add the carrot and celery and cook for 3 minutes, allowing them to cook yet remain tender. Add the turmeric, ginger, black pepper, and cayenne and stir until the vegetables are fully coated with the spices.

3. Increase the heat to medium-high, add the broth, and bring the mixture to a boil. Once mixture is boiling, reduce the heat to low and add cauliflower and zucchini. Cover the saucepan and simmer for 15 to 20 minutes, until the cauliflower is very tender.

4. Stir in the kale and cannellini beans and cook for 1 to 2 minutes more, until the greens are slightly wilted. Serve hot.

# Braised Chicken
## with Lemon and Artichoke

**Serves 4**

(GF)

This artichoke- and olive-infused chicken is pepped up by cancer-fighting lemon zest, while coriander and cumin provide synergistic antioxidant effects that are further boosted by cinnamon. You can also make it completely vegan by eliminating the chicken entirely and doubling the amount of chickpeas.

4 boneless, skinless, organic free-range chicken breasts or thighs (about 2 pounds)

Sea salt and freshly ground black pepper

**3 tablespoons** extra-virgin olive oil

**1 medium** yellow onion, diced (about 2 cups)

**4** garlic cloves, thinly sliced

**1 teaspoon** ground turmeric

**1 teaspoon** crushed red pepper flakes

**½ teaspoon** ground cumin

**½ teaspoon** ground coriander

**¼ teaspoon** ground cinnamon

**1** bay leaf

**2½ cups** low-sodium chicken or vegetable broth

**1 tablespoon** freshly grated lemon zest (from 1 medium lemon)

**3 tablespoons** freshly squeezed lemon juice (from 1 medium lemon)

**1½ cups** cooked chickpeas, drained and rinsed

**2 cups** artichoke hearts, thawed from frozen

**½ cup** pitted green olives (optional)

**2 tablespoons** chopped fresh cilantro, for garnish

**1.** Season the chicken with salt and black pepper on both sides. Heat the oil over medium-high heat in a Dutch oven. Add half of the chicken pieces and cook until browned on each side, 3 to 4 minutes per side. Transfer to a plate and repeat with the remaining chicken.

**2.** Reduce the heat to medium, add the onion and garlic to the saucepan, and cook for 4 to 5 minutes, until the onion is softened and golden. Add the turmeric, red pepper flakes, cumin, coriander, cinnamon, and bay leaf and cook, stirring constantly, for 1 minute.

**3.** Add ½ cup of the broth to deglaze the saucepan slightly and season with salt to taste. Continue to cook over medium heat for 5 minutes until the liquid is reduced by half.

**4.** Add the remaining 2 cups of broth, lemon zest, and lemon juice. Reduce the heat to medium-low, cover, and let simmer for 15 minutes.

**5.** Add the chicken, chickpeas, artichoke hearts, and olives (if using) and stir gently to combine. Increase the heat to medium-high, cover, and simmer for 5 to 10 minutes more, stirring occasionally, until the chicken is cooked through. Garnish with the cilantro and serve.

# Sizzling Up Your Sides

Side dishes are a great way to add variety and nutritional power to your meal, but many people miss out on this opportunity by choosing sides that are full of refined carbs and rely on plain old salt and pepper. Not anymore! These easy side dishes feature a variety of textures and unique spice combinations that are sure to impress, whether you're enjoying a quiet meal at home or filling up a party platter for guests.

# Spiced Parsnip and Sweet Potato Coins

**Serves 8**

Studies have shown that the combination of cardamom and black pepper may boost the action of cancer-fighting cells in our body. This dish also pairs cardamom with cinnamon and ginger, which are delightfully aromatic and help fight heart disease. These parsnips and sweet potatoes are the perfect balance of sweet and spicy, and I often enjoy them as an afternoon snack on their own with some walnuts. They also shine alongside a simple chicken or bean dish or tossed into a lunchtime salad.

**3 medium** sweet potatoes, cut into ¼-inch thick rounds (about 5 cups)

**4 medium** parsnips, peeled and cut into ¼-inch thick rounds (about 4 cups)

**3 tablespoons** extra-virgin olive oil

**1 teaspoon** ground cinnamon*

**½ teaspoon** ground ginger*

**¼ teaspoon** ground cardamom

Sea salt and freshly ground black pepper to taste

*Sub spices for: **1 teaspoon** CinnaPeel Breakfast Blend (page 52) plus **¼ teaspoon** cardamom and pinch of black pepper*

**1.** Preheat the oven to 400°F and line a rimmed baking sheet with parchment paper.

**2.** Toss the sweet potatoes and parsnips with the oil, cinnamon, ginger, and cardamom on the baking sheet; season with salt and pepper.

**3.** Roast for 30 to 35 minutes, until the vegetables are fork-tender. Serve immediately, as they keep their full crunch for the first hour and then start to slightly soften. You can refrigerate leftovers in an airtight container for 2 to 3 days.

# Za'atar-Roasted Cauliflower

Serves 6

1 **medium** head cauliflower, cored and cut into mini florets (about 4 cups)

3 **tablespoons** extra-virgin olive oil

1½ **tablespoons** za'atar

1 **teaspoon** paprika

½ **teaspoon** ground cumin

Sea salt and freshly ground black pepper to taste

Cauliflower is a vegetable that soaks up the flavor of whatever coats it. My favorite addition is the traditional za'atar spice blend. This is the condiment king of Middle Eastern cuisine. It typically contains thyme, oregano, and marjoram along with sumac and toasted sesame seeds, which come together to create a tangy, nutty, and slightly woodsy flavor. This combo also exerts major antibacterial and antioxidant effects (people in the Middle East have used it to eliminate parasites since ancient times). I use it to eliminate taste-bud boredom!

1. Preheat the oven to 400°F and line a rimmed baking sheet with parchment paper.

2. In a large bowl, combine the cauliflower, oil, za'atar, paprika, cumin, and salt and pepper and toss to coat the cauliflower evenly.

3. Transfer the cauliflower to the prepared baking sheet, spreading the florets in an even layer, and roast for 15 minutes. Remove the baking sheet from the oven and toss the cauliflower to ensure even cooking. Return it to the oven and roast for 30 minutes more, or until cauliflower is nicely browned all over. Serve immediately.

# Ruby Red Beet Salad

**Serves 4 to 6**

(V) (GF)

Each bite of this chilled salad is loaded with color and antioxidants. The rich pigments that give beets their bright color are called betalains, which have been studied for their anticancer abilities. While these compounds shine on their own, they're supplemented here with the digestion-enhancing properties of cumin and black pepper, as well as the brightness from lemon and fresh herbs. It's a perfect complement to a light salad; I love it with the Lentil Salad with Spicy Vinaigrette (page 95).

**6 medium** red beets (about 1 ½ pounds)

**3 tablespoons** freshly squeezed lemon juice (from about 1 lemon)

**2½ tablespoons** extra-virgin olive oil

**1** garlic clove, minced (optional)

**½ cup** chopped fresh parsley or cilantro

**½ teaspoon** ground cumin

Sea salt and freshly ground black pepper to taste

**1.** In a medium saucepan over medium-high heat, bring 8 cups of water to a boil. Add the beets, reduce the heat to low, and cook for 30 to 40 minutes, until the beets are tender when pierced with a fork. Drain the beets in a colander and leave them to cool.

**2.** When the beets are cool enough to handle, peel each one under cold running water. Transfer the beets to a cutting board and slice them or cut them into medium-size cubes. In a medium bowl, combine the beets, lemon juice, olive oil, garlic (if using), parsley, and cumin and lightly toss. Season with salt and pepper and refrigerate in a sealed container for at least an hour before serving. Serve chilled.

# Herbs Galore Farro

**Serves 4**

(vo)

Farro is a perfectly chewy, nutty ancient grain that's packed with protein and fiber. This salad uses the Beller Basic Vinaigrette (page 133) to make it super flavorful. It's great warm or chilled—I always double this recipe and find that it stays tender and delicious stored in the refrigerator for days. I love it as a pre-workout snack, and I even eat it for breakfast en route to work (I add a tablespoon of chia seeds for more fiber). It gives the body a flavorful boost of energy and satisfies without being too heavy.

**1 cup** farro

**2½ cups** low-sodium chicken or vegetable broth

**⅓ cup** Beller Basic Vinaigrette (page 133)

**2 cups** coarsely chopped fresh mint or cilantro

**2 cups** coarsely chopped fresh parsley

**12** green olives, pitted and sliced (optional)

**1.** In a medium saucepan, combine the farro, salt, and broth (or water) over medium-high heat. Reduce heat and bring to a simmer, cover, and cook, stirring occasionally, for 35 to 45 minutes, until the farro is tender. (You want it to be a little firm, so check it a few times while cooking.)

**2.** Remove the saucepan from the heat and drain any excess water. Add the vinaigrette, fresh herbs, and olives (if using) to the farro and toss until well combined. Serve warm or chilled; it can be stored in an airtight container in the refrigerator for up to 3 days.

# Zesty Zucchini Salad

**Serves 4 to 6**

I was surprised that this super-refreshing summer salad tastes even better as left-overs! The combination of sumac and citrus will brighten up your day, while the zest from the citrus fruits boosts your health with anticancer flavonoids. You can use either a mandoline or a simple vegetable peeler to create the thin ribbons of zucchini and carrot, which appear almost pasta-like. Since this salad is served raw, be sure to use cold-pressed extra-virgin olive oil, which is even more flavorful than standard olive oil.

**1** garlic clove, minced

**1 teaspoon** freshly grated lemon zest (from about ½ lemon)

**3 tablespoons** freshly squeezed lemon juice (from about 1 lemon)

**3 tablespoons** freshly squeezed lime juice (from about 2 limes)

**4 tablespoons** cold-pressed extra-virgin olive oil

**2 teaspoons** ground sumac

Sea salt and freshly ground black pepper to taste

**4 medium** green or yellow zucchini (6 to 8 ounces), sliced into thin ribbons

**2 medium** carrots, sliced into thin ribbons

**3 tablespoons** finely chopped fresh mint

**½ cup** finely chopped fresh parsley

Crushed red pepper flakes

**1.** In a medium bowl, combine the garlic, lemon zest and juice, lime juice, oil, sumac, and salt and pepper and whisk until well blended.

**2.** Add the zucchini and carrots to the bowl and use your hands to massage the dressing into the strips until well coated.

**3.** Stir in the mint and parsley and sprinkle with red pepper flakes. Cover the bowl and let the zucchini and carrots marinate for 10 minutes in the refrigerator before serving either chilled or at room temperature.

# Warm Fennel Salad

**Serves 4**

(V) (GF)

Feeling a little bloated? Fennel and parsley are my secret ingredients for helping my clients (and now you) get red-carpet ready, since they both help flush extra fluids out of your system. Roasted fennel has a smooth, mild flavor that makes this a true comfort food experience. This recipe is a well-loved dish in my house, since it's so quick to prepare. Just slice, spice, roast, and done! You can pair this with just about any main dish, or do what I do and eat it straight out of the oven.

2 fennel bulbs (about 2 pounds), halved lengthwise and sliced crosswise ¼ inch thick

1½ **tablespoons** extra-virgin olive oil or avocado oil

½ **teaspoon** ground turmeric

¼ **teaspoon** crushed red pepper flakes or cayenne

Sea salt and freshly ground pepper to taste

½ **cup** chopped fresh parsley

3 **tablespoons** freshly squeezed lemon juice (from about 1 lemon)

**1.** Preheat the oven to 425°F and line a rimmed baking sheet with parchment paper.

**2.** Combine the fennel, oil, turmeric, red pepper flakes, and salt and pepper on the prepared baking sheet and toss until the fennel is evenly coated.

**3.** Roast for 20 to 25 minutes, until the fennel is tender and lightly browned around the edges.

**4.** Transfer the fennel to a serving bowl and toss with the chopped parsley and lemon juice. Serve warm.

# Spiced-Up Crispy Chickpeas

**Makes 3 cups**

Ever see those crispy chickpea snacks all packaged up in the grocery aisle? I always pass them by, because some are loaded with sugars, fillers, and preservatives. Here's a recipe that's not only way cheaper but also flexible enough to switch up, depending on what flavors you're craving! The anti-inflammatory Vegitude version is a staple at my house, but I also love keeping the more savory chili version around as a snack. To make this into a meal, serve either warm or at room temperature over a bed of greens with a drizzle of Beller Basic Vinaigrette (page 133). I occasionally sub out the chickpeas for edamame just to mix it up.

**3 cups** cooked chickpeas (or edamame), rinsed and drained (see page 45)

**2 tablespoons** extra-virgin olive oil

Spice blend of choice (see below)

Sea salt and freshly ground black pepper to taste

**FOR BLEND OPTION #1:**
**3 TEASPOONS VEGGIE POWER-UP BLEND (PAGE 52), OR**

**1 teaspoon** granulated garlic

**1 teaspoon** granulated onion

**1 teaspoon** ground turmeric

**½ teaspoon** dried parsley

**FOR BLEND OPTION #2:**
**2 TEASPOONS EVERYTHING SAVORY POWER BLEND (PAGE 52) PLUS ¼ TEASPOON CAYENNE, OR**

**1 teaspoon** sweet paprika

**½ teaspoon** garlic powder

**½ teaspoon** ground turmeric

**¼ teaspoon** ground cumin

**¼ teaspoon** cayenne

**FOR BLEND OPTION #3:**
**2 TEASPOONS CHILI POWDER**

1. Preheat the oven to 400°F and line a rimmed baking sheet with parchment paper.

2. In a medium bowl, toss the chickpeas (or edamame, if using) with the oil and preferred spices and season with salt and pepper.

3. Spread the chickpeas in a single layer on the prepared baking sheet and roast for 25 to 30 minutes, until golden brown. Turn off the oven and leave the baking sheet inside until cool; this step is optional but it makes them crispier.

4. Refrigerate the chickpeas in an airtight jar for up to 5 days.

# Immune Support Yellow Quinoa

## with Parsley and Almonds

**Serves 2 or 3**

Quinoa has become a favorite of health food junkies, and for good reason—it's a complete protein and full of fiber, and it can be prepared soft and fluffy or firm and crunchy, depending on your mood. Resist the urge to serve quinoa plain, since you can exponentially boost your anti-inflammatory, blood-sugar-regulating benefits in a snap. You may not automatically think to pair turmeric with cumin and cinnamon, but trust me—once you make this, you won't go back to spiceless monotony! If you don't have parsley and almonds, they can easily be either omitted or replaced with other nuts and herbs you have on hand.

**1 tablespoon** extra-virgin olive oil or avocado oil

**1 medium** yellow onion, diced (about 2 cups)

**1 teaspoon** ground turmeric

**½ teaspoon** ground cumin

**½ teaspoon** ground cinnamon

**¼ teaspoon** sea salt

**¼ teaspoon** freshly ground black pepper

**1 cup** (uncooked) quinoa

**½ cup** finely chopped fresh parsley

**¼ cup** sliced raw almonds

**1 cup** shredded carrots (about 1 large carrot; optional)

**1.** Heat the oil in a medium saucepan over medium heat. When the oil is shimmering, add the onion and cook for 3 to 5 minutes, until translucent.

**2.** Add the turmeric, cumin, and cinnamon, and season with the salt and pepper. Stir well for about 30 seconds, or until the spices are fragrant.

**3.** Add 2 cups water and the quinoa to the saucepan and bring to a boil. Cover, reduce the heat to low, and cook for 15 minutes.

**4.** Remove the saucepan from the heat and fluff the quinoa with a fork. Stir the parsley, almonds, and shredded carrots (if using) into the quinoa and serve warm or chilled.

**5.** Store leftovers in an airtight container for up to 4 days.

# Dressings and Dips

**As the saying goes, the secret is in the sauce—especially if spices are involved.** These dips and dressings are loaded with spices and low in sugar to help make your salads, crudités, and other side dishes deliciously powerful. I suggest having at least one of these dressings on hand throughout the week, since this makes adding a dollop of goodness to your meals that much easier. Many of these recipes use a blender; if you don't have one or if you prefer an even quicker prep route, you can just as easily combine all the ingredients in a jar and shake it for 30 to 40 seconds, until everything is incorporated. Go ahead, whip up a batch, and take advantage of every spicing opportunity!

# Turmeric Tahini Dip

**Makes ⅔ cup**

(V) (GF)

Rich and tangy with a vibrant infusion of turmeric, this anti-inflammatory dip is perfect when scooped up with fresh or roasted vegetables. My clients often enjoy it as a sandwich spread, as a mayo substitute in egg salad, or drizzled on Za'atar-Roasted Cauliflower (page 118). You can also use it to dress up a salad made with red-leaf lettuce, kale, or arugula. These greens are rich in quercetin, which boosts absorption of turmeric for an extra-powerful anti-inflammatory boost.

**½ cup** tahini

**¼ cup plus 1 tablespoon** freshly squeezed lemon juice (from about 2 lemons)

**¼ cup** extra-virgin olive oil

**1** garlic clove

**1 teaspoon** ground turmeric

**½ teaspoon** cayenne

**½ teaspoon** ground fenugreek (optional)

**⅛ teaspoon** freshly ground black pepper

Sea salt to taste

**2 tablespoons** chopped fresh parsley, for topping (optional)

Harissa, for serving (optional)

**1.** In a blender, combine the tahini, lemon juice, oil, garlic, turmeric, cayenne, fenugreek (if using), black pepper, and ½ cup water and blend until smooth. Taste and season with salt. If the mixture seems too thick, slowly add a little more water and pulse again until it reaches the desired consistency.

**2.** Serve immediately with parsley and harissa, if desired, or pour the dip into an airtight container and store for up to 5 days in the refrigerator.

# Spicy Vinaigrette

**Makes 1 cup**

(V) (GF)

I religiously make a batch of lentils on Sunday night, because it's my standard vegan protein to have on hand during the busy workweek. This vinaigrette, however, is anything but standard and is one of my favorite ways to dress up Lentil Salad (page 95) and add some delicious variety to my lunch routine. This vinaigrette is great on any veggies or greens—super versatile and a great option when you just want an extra kick of both spice and antioxidants!

⅔ **cup** extra-virgin olive oil

¼ **cup** red wine vinegar

¼ **cup** freshly squeezed lemon juice (from about 2 lemons)

½ **teaspoon** granulated garlic

**1 teaspoon** ground cumin

½ **teaspoon** cayenne

Sea salt to taste

¼ **teaspoon** freshly ground black pepper

¼ **teaspoon** ground coriander (optional)

¼ **teaspoon** ground fenugreek (optional)

**1.** In a blender, combine the oil, vinegar, lemon juice, garlic, cumin, cayenne, a pinch of salt, pepper, and the coriander and fenugreek (if using) and blend on low speed until smooth. Season with additional salt to taste.

**2.** Serve immediately, or pour the vinaigrette into an airtight container and store for up to 5 days in the refrigerator (shake the container before serving to re-incorporate the ingredients).

# Green Goddess Fenugreek Tahini Sauce

**Makes 2 cups**

Green goddess dressing is a California classic, but it typically includes mayo, which makes for a heftier sauce than your salad needs. This version uses tahini, the silky sesame-seed paste that's full of healthy fats, and includes a hefty dose of detoxifying, debloating herbs—as well as cancer-fighting fenugreek. This thick, creamy dressing makes a wonderful dip for crudités or falafel (page 109), or it can be massaged into a kale salad.

**2** garlic cloves, crushed

**¾ cup** chopped fresh cilantro

**¾ cup** chopped fresh parsley

**1 teaspoon** ground cumin

**1 teaspoon** ground fenugreek

**2 teaspoons** sea salt, plus more to taste

**1 cup** tahini

**¼ cup plus 1 tablespoon** freshly squeezed lemon juice (from about 2 lemons)

**1.** In a food processor, combine the garlic, cilantro, parsley, cumin, fenugreek, and salt and process for about 30 seconds, or until the texture resembles that of pesto. Add the tahini, 1 cup water, and lemon juice and pulse for 45 seconds more. Add additional water, if desired, to thin out the sauce until it reaches your desired consistency, and season with additional salt to taste.

**2.** Serve immediately or pour the sauce into an airtight container and store for up to 5 days in the refrigerator.

# Beller Basic Vinaigrette

**Makes 1 cup**

(V) (GF)

I always have a jar of this in my fridge—once you make it, you'll never choose a store-bought bottle again. Making your own vinaigrette takes about 5 minutes and is so worth it, both for your health and for the superior flavor profile. Instead of pro-inflammatory oils that are standard in store-bought versions, this recipe uses extra-virgin olive oil, which not only helps fights inflammation but also helps reduce the risk of cardiovascular disease. As opposed to standard vinaigrettes, this one is spiced with cumin and crushed red pepper flakes for an extra calorie-burning boost. Use this vinaigrette on the Herbs Galore Farro (page 121) or on your favorite go-to salad—it's a universal dressing that you can feel great about reaching for day after day!

¼ **cup plus 2 tablespoons** extra-virgin olive oil

3 **tablespoons** balsamic vinegar

2 **tablespoons** Dijon mustard

¼ **cup** freshly squeezed lemon juice (from about 2 lemons)

3 **tablespoons** minced shallots

¼ **teaspoon** ground cumin

¼ **teaspoon** crushed red pepper flakes

¼ **teaspoon** freshly ground black pepper

Sea salt to taste

1. In a blender, combine the oil, vinegar, mustard, lemon juice, shallots, cumin, red pepper flakes, pepper, and a pinch of salt and blend on low speed until smooth. Season with additional salt to taste.

2. Serve immediately or transfer the vinaigrette to an airtight container and store for up to 5 days in the refrigerator (shake the container before serving to re-incorporate the ingredients).

# Chimichurri Sauce

**Makes 2 cups**

(V) (GF)

This herbaceous Argentinian sauce is innately antioxidant heavy due to generous amounts of fresh herbs and spices! While chimichurri is typically served with steak, I recommend using it as a topping for fish (such as the Simple Weeknight Salmon with Chimichurri on page 97), sautéed mushrooms, steamed broccoli, onions, spinach, eggs . . . any dish that would benefit from a fresh herb flavor!

¼ **cup** red wine vinegar

2 **cups** chopped fresh Italian parsley

¼ **cup** chopped fresh oregano, or
  1 **tablespoon** dried

1 shallot, minced

3 garlic cloves, minced

1 **teaspoon** paprika

2 **teaspoons** crushed red pepper flakes

½ **teaspoon** freshly ground black pepper

½ **teaspoon** sea salt

¾ **cup** extra-virgin olive oil

**1.** In a medium bowl, combine the vinegar, parsley, oregano, shallot, garlic, paprika, red pepper flakes, black pepper, and salt and stir until well blended.

**2.** Transfer the mixture to an airtight container and whisk in the olive oil. Refrigerate for at least 1 hour before serving to allow the flavors to combine.

**3.** The chimichurri will stay fresh in the refrigerator for up to a week (stir before serving to re-incorporate the ingredients).

# Vegan Caesar Dressing

**Makes ¾ cups**

(V) (GF)

Caesar dressing is typically made with anchovy, egg, and Parmesan cheese. My family loves Caesar salads, but both my husband and the kids gobbled up this guilt-free vegan version without even real- izing it was plant based. It really is that indulgent! Hidden in this dressing are antioxidant-packed ingredients like lemon zest, turmeric, and cayenne. To add even more health benefits, go beyond the classic Romaine and try drizzling this dressing over a plate of baby spinach and arugula instead, or of course you can use this in the Vegan Creamy Brussels Sprout Caesar (page 106).

**¼ cup plus 1 tablespoon** avocado oil or extra-virgin olive oil

**1 teaspoon** freshly grated lemon zest

**3 tablespoons** freshly squeezed lemon juice (from about 1 large lemon)

**2** garlic cloves, minced

**1 tablespoon** Dijon mustard

**2 teaspoons** tamari

**½ teaspoon** ground turmeric, or **1 teaspoon** Veggie Power-Up Blend (page 52)

**⅛ teaspoon** crushed red pepper flakes or cayenne

**1.** In a blender, combine the oil, lemon zest, lemon juice, garlic, mustard, tamari, turmeric, and red pepper flakes and blend on low until smooth.

**2.** Serve immediately or pour the dressing into an airtight container and store for up to 5 days in the refrigerator.

# Snacks and Sweets

**That's right, snacks are *mandatory* in my book.** There are too many hours between lunch and dinner—and sometimes between dinner and bedtime—to not eat between meals at all. You'll get cravings, and cravings lead to junk food. I also understand we all have a sweet tooth that demands attention, and denying it may only enhance those urges. These spicy and sweet snacks and desserts are low on effort and high on flavor, to appease all your cravings and urges.

# Hummus 3 Ways (or More!)

**Makes 2 cups**

After making this, you'll never settle for store-bought hummus again! Think of hummus as a blank canvas in which to stir in a wide range of flavorful spices. By making your own, you also get to control the quality of oil in the hummus (store-bought versions are usually made with cheap, pro-inflammatory oils) and ditch the preservatives. My go-to spices to sprinkle on top or mix into hummus are the antioxidant-rich combination of cumin and paprika; za'atar for its distinctly Middle Eastern flavor; sumac for a smoky-lemony twist; or saffron for its rich, beautiful color. I also regularly stir in the Everything Savory Power Blend (page 52), the Veggie Power-Up Blend (page 52), and the Moroccan Roll Blend (page 53).

**2 cups** cooked chickpeas, rinsed and drained (see page 45)

**1** garlic clove

**3 tablespoons** extra-virgin olive oil

**¼ cup** freshly squeezed lemon juice (from about 2 lemons), plus more as needed

**½ cup** tahini

**½ teaspoon** ground cumin

Sea salt to taste

**1 tablespoon** za'atar or ground sumac, or **½ to 1 teaspoon** saffron (see Note)

Extra-virgin olive oil, for finishing

Chopped fresh parsley, for garnish

**Pinch** of paprika, for garnish

**1.** In a food processor or blender, combine the chickpeas, garlic, oil, lemon juice, tahini, and cumin and process until fully incorporated. Season with salt to taste.

**2.** Add 2 to 3 tablespoons water, a tablespoon at a time, and pulse again until it reaches the desired consistency. Season with more salt as needed. Stir in the za'atar (or sumac or saffron). Add more lemon juice, if desired.

**3.** To serve, transfer the hummus to a small serving bowl, drizzle with the olive oil, and sprinkle with parsley and paprika.

**NOTE** *For the saffron version of this hummus, soak ½ teaspoon of saffron threads in 2 tablespoons of warm water for 5 minutes; add the saffron and water mix before serving as indicated below.*

# Frozen 'Nana "Sandwiches"

**Serves 2**

(V) (GF)

These creamy frozen treats are coming in hot! My teen clients especially love this recipe as an after-school snack, while my friends enjoy them as a healthy dessert—regardless, it's a great nutritional opportunity to add the power of spices to your daily routine. My favorite spice additions are a few shakes of the CinnaPeel Breakfast Blend and raw cacao powder, but feel free to get creative! You can amp up nut butter in so many ways—see some ideas on page 48.

**2 tablespoons** almond butter or your favorite nut butter

**2 small** bananas, halved lengthwise

Cacao powder

Several dashes of ground cinnamon*

*Sub: **several dashes** CinnaPeel Breakfast Blend (page 52) or Golden Power Breakfast Blend (page 52)

**1.**   Spread half of the nut butter on one banana half and sprinkle with cacao and cinnamon as desired. Place a second banana half on top of the first to create a "sandwich." Repeat with the remaining banana.

**2.**   Wrap each banana sandwich in parchment paper and place them in a large ziplock bag or airtight container. Freeze for at least 1 hour.

**3.**   When you're ready for a snack, remove the sandwiches from the freezer and simply slice each one into smaller pieces. These will keep in the freezer for up to 3 months.

# Popped Sorghum (or Popcorn) Your Way

**Serves 1**

A movie without popcorn is unacceptable in my book—but don't settle for the butter-doused type from the theaters. This version with sorghum can be adapted to whatever flavor you're craving. Sorghum is a high-fiber, gluten-free grain that's wonderfully satisfying and crunchy. You can easily use organic popcorn kernels instead of sorghum, if you prefer. Either way, here both the sweet and savory versions are packed with major cancer-fighting spices! If you don't feel like measuring anything, you can simply sprinkle some za'atar or paprika, granulated garlic, turmeric, and freshly ground black pepper on top of the kernels as you please.

**2 tablespoons** avocado oil, extra-virgin olive oil, or coconut oil

**¼ cup** sorghum or organic corn kernels

Sea salt to taste

Spice blend of choice (see below)

**FOR BLEND OPTION #1:
SWEET WITH HEAT**

**1 tablespoon** cacao powder

**Pinch** of ground cinnamon

**Pinch** of cayenne

**FOR BLEND OPTION #2:
CHEESY AND SAVORY**

**2 tablespoons** nutritional yeast

**1 teaspoon** Everything Savory Power Blend (page 52)

**1.** Heat the oil in a medium saucepan over medium-high heat. When the oil is shimmering, add 3 or 4 kernels to the pot. Once they start to pop, add the remaining kernels to the saucepan and cover, gently shaking the pot occasionally to prevent the kernels from burning. Continue to cook until most of the kernels have popped and you can no longer hear them moving against the bottom of the saucepan.

**2.** Remove the saucepan from the heat and continue to shake in order to pop any remaining kernels. Carefully remove the lid and transfer the sorghum to a bowl.

**3.** Toss with salt and the spice blend of your choice while the sorghum is still warm and serve.

---

**TIP** *Pop only small amounts (i.e. no more than a ¼ cup) at a time. Sorghum kernels will pop better when they have more room in the pot.*

# Vegan Chocolate Truffles

**Makes twenty-four 1-inch truffles**

These are chocolate truffles that you don't have to feel guilty about. The natural sweetness of dates is balanced by the healthy fats in the nuts and coconut flakes, fiber from the chia seeds, and antidiabetic effects of cacao so your blood sugars won't go on a roller coaster ride. While the cayenne in this recipe is optional, I strongly recommend it, as its anticancer power boosts alongside cacao, and a little spice in chocolate is always delicious. These truffles make a great treat for your special someone, but treating yourself to a batch isn't a bad idea either!

**1 cup** dried Medjool dates, pitted (about 10)

**¾ cup** raw, unsalted almonds, or your favorite raw nuts

**2 tablespoons** cacao powder

**⅛ teaspoon** cayenne (optional)

**1 tablespoon** chia seeds

**½ cup** unsweetened coconut flakes

**Pinch** of sea salt

**1.** In a bowl, cover the dates with warm water to soak for about 5 minutes, or until they have plumped slightly. Meanwhile, line a rimmed baking sheet with parchment paper and set it aside.

**2.** Drain the dates (discard the water) and transfer them to a food processor. Add the almonds, cacao, cayenne (if using), chia seeds, coconut flakes, and salt and pulse about 5 to 6 times until the mixture resembles a thick paste.

**3.** Scoop out 1 tablespoon of the truffle mixture and, using your hands, roll it into a 1-inch ball. Place the truffle on the baking sheet and repeat with the remaining mixture; you should have 24 truffles. Cover with a sheet of parchment paper and refrigerate the truffles for at least 2 hours, or until firm.

**4.** Remove the truffles from the refrigerator and serve, or transfer them to an airtight container, where they will keep for up to 1 week in the refrigerator. They also freeze well and can be kept frozen for 2 months.

# Spiced Nut and Date Bars

**Makes 12 bars**

The only processing going into these bars is via your food processor. They are nothing like the energy and granola bars found at grocery stores, many of which contain brown rice syrup and other added sweeteners, soy isolates, and miscellaneous synthetic ingredients—no, thank you! With plenty of nuts and dried fruit, these bars instead pack a healthy dose of protein and, of course, a flavorful health boost from ginger, cinnamon, and cardamom. When it comes to quick, portable snacks or breakfast options, these bars can't be beat!

**1 cup** dried Medjool dates, pitted (about 10)

**1 cup** raw, unsalted almonds

**1 cup** raw, unsalted cashews

**1 tablespoon** ground cinnamon

**½ teaspoon** ground ginger

**⅛ teaspoon** ground cardamom

**1 teaspoon** pure vanilla extract

**Pinch** of sea salt

**1 cup** roughly chopped dried apricots or apple rings (sulfur-free, no-sugar-added varieties)

**2 tablespoons** chia seeds

**1.** In a bowl, cover the dates with warm water to soak for about 5 minutes, or until they have plumped slightly; drain. Line the bottom of an 8 × 8-inch baking dish with parchment paper and set it aside.

**2.** In a food processor, combine the almonds and cashews and pulse for 15 to 20 seconds, until the nuts are chopped into small pieces. Add the dates, cinnamon, ginger, cardamom, vanilla, and salt and pulse for 35 to 40 seconds, until the mixture resembles a thick paste. If the mixture is sticking to the sides or bottom of the food processor, add up to 2 teaspoons water, a little at a time, and pulse again until all of the ingredients are well combined. Add the dried fruit and chia seeds and pulse for 20 seconds more.

**3.** Use a spatula to transfer the mixture from the food processor to the prepared baking dish, and spread it into an even layer, pressing it with the spatula. Refrigerate 6 to 8 hours, or up to overnight, as it will allow the mixture to become firm for cutting.

**4.** Remove the baking dish from the refrigerator and cut the mixture into 12 bars. Eat right away, or store them in an airtight container in the refrigerator for up to 1 week. They freeze well and can be kept frozen for 2 months.

# Chai-Poached Pears

**Serves 4 to 8**

(V) (GF)

This recipe has my mother's name written all over it! She makes a batch weekly and uses it as an oatmeal topping or a sweet snack or dessert (she eats it both chilled and warm). When you want to treat your friends, this dessert will show how much you really care about them. It's decadent and feels oh-so-fancy for either a weeknight get-together or a long-weekend evening. Little do they know how simple the prep is, nor will they guess that their dessert is fighting heart disease, cooling inflammation, and soothing the digestive system all at once. If you don't have pears on hand, crisp apples (such as Golden Delicious or Gala) are a tasty substitution.

**1 tablespoon** ground cinnamon, plus more (optional) for sprinkling

**1 (1-inch)** piece fresh ginger, thinly sliced

¼ **teaspoon** ground cardamom, or 10 pods, crushed

**4 medium** pears or apples (any variety), halved lengthwise

1. Preheat the oven to 350°F.

2. Pour 4 cups water into an 8 × 8-inch glass or ceramic baking dish and using a spoon, stir in the cinnamon along with the ginger and cardamom. Arrange the pears cut side down into the baking dish. Bake about 1 hour, or until the pears are fork-tender and lightly browned. Sprinkle with additional cinnamon, if desired, and serve. Serve warm or chilled. Store them in an airtight container in the refrigerator for up to 1 week.

# Mexican Chili-Lime Fruit Salad

**Serves 6**

If you've been to Los Angeles, you've probably noticed Mexican fruit carts on many street corners. Parking is the worst in LA, but when my kids point to one of the fruit carts, I make sure to find a spot and pull over—it's totally worth it. They sell a variety of tropical fruit seasoned with fresh lime juice and chili powder. Sweet, tangy, and spicy, it hits all of the right notes. Here's my version that you can easily toss together at home—the chili powder upgrades the fruit with a tangy antioxidant punch!

**6 cups** sliced fruit (any combination of mango, watermelon, strawberries, blueberries, and/or pineapple; jicama and cucumber also taste great)

**2 tablespoons** freshly squeezed lime juice (from about 2 limes)

**¼ teaspoon** chili powder

**Pinch** of sea salt, plus more to taste

In a large bowl, combine the fruit with the lime juice, chili, and salt and gently toss until the fruit is evenly coated. Taste, adjust seasonings as desired, and serve.

# Chocolate Date "Nice Cream"

**Serves 1**

(V) (GF)

Are you screaming for ice cream? Whip up this delicious and indulgent dessert before your voice gets hoarse. This chocolaty treat takes only 2 minutes to make and uses just four pantry ingredients, but it's absolutely packed with antioxidants due to a whole tablespoon of cacao powder. The date adds a touch of natural sweetness and healthy B vitamins, while the fresh raspberries pair beautifully with the dark chocolate flavor and add a splash of cheerful color.

**1 small** ripe banana, frozen

**1 tablespoon** cacao powder

**¾ cup** non-dairy milk

**1** dried Medjoal date, pitted

**¼ cup** fresh raspberries, for serving

1. In a blender, combine the banana, cacao, milk, and date and blend until smooth.

2. Transfer the mixture to a small bowl, top with raspberries, and serve.

# Appendix: Spices and Health Benefits

| Recipes | Cancer Fighting | Heart Healthy | Brain Boosting | Anti-Inflammatory |
|---|:---:|:---:|:---:|:---:|
| CinnaPeel Breakfast Blend, p. 52 | • | • | • | • |
| Golden Power Breakfast Blend, p. 52 | • | • | • | • |
| Everything Savory Power Blend, p. 52 | • | • | • | • |
| Veggie Power-Up Blend, p. 52 | • | | • | • |
| Moroccan Roll Blend, p. 53 | • | • | • | • |
| Sweet Success Morning Blend, p. 53 | • | • | • | • |
| Tex-Mex Power Blend, p. 53 | • | • | • | • |
| Rachel's Anti-Cancer Power Tonic, p. 57 | • | • | • | • |
| Turkish Waker-Upper Coffee, p. 58 | • | • | • | • |
| Stabilizing Matcha, p. 61 | • | • | • | • |
| Soothing Matcha, p. 61 | • | • | • | • |
| Prevention Matcha, p. 61 | • | • | • | • |
| Red-Hot Chili Cocoa, p. 62 | • | • | • | • |
| Immunity Shot, p. 65 | • | | | • |
| Digestion Booster Shot, p. 65 | • | • | | |
| Metabolism Revving Shot, p. 65 | • | | | • |
| Saffron and Cardamom Latte, p. 66 | • | • | • | • |
| Bedtime Recovery Tea, p. 69 | • | • | • | • |
| Spiced Zucchini Almond Muffins, p. 71 | • | • | • | • |
| Power-Spiced Overnight Oats, p. 72 | • | • | • | • |
| Butternut Squash and Apple Bake, p. 75 | • | • | • | • |
| Banana Silver Dollar Pancakes, p. 76 | • | • | • | • |
| Cinnamon-Quinoa Granola, p. 79 | • | • | • | • |
| Spiced Sweet Potato Pockets, p. 80 | • | • | • | • |
| Fiesta Scramble, p. 83 | • | • | • | • |
| Apple-Zested Muesli, p. 84 | • | • | • | • |
| Savory Sorghum Porridge, p. 87 | • | • | • | • |
| Chickpea Shakshuka, p. 88 | • | • | • | • |
| Israeli Breakfast Sampler, p. 91 | • | • | | • |
| Tzimmes Oat Crumble, p. 92 | • | • | | • |
| Lentil Salad with Spicy Vinaigrette, p. 95 | • | • | | • |
| Simple Weeknight Salmon with Chimichurri, p. 97 | • | • | • | • |
| Black Bean Choco Chili, p. 98 | • | • | • | • |
| Glowing Green Frittata, p. 101 | • | • | • | • |
| Moroccan Chicken Stew, p. 102 | • | • | • | • |
| Anti-inflammatory Chickpea Curry, p. 105 | • | • | • | • |
| Vegan Creamy Brussels Sprout Caesar, p. 106 | • | • | • | • |
| Baked Falafel with Green Goddess Fenugreek Tahini Sauce, p. 109 | • | • | • | • |
| Spiced Crispy Tofu, p. 110 | • | • | • | • |
| Tex-Mex Wraps, p. 111 | • | • | • | • |
| Immunity Turmeric Soup, p. 112 | • | • | • | • |
| Braised Chicken with Lemon and Artichoke, p. 114 | • | • | • | • |

| Good for the Gut | Helps Digestion | Immune Boosting | Promotes Weight Loss | Bloat Reducing | Detoxifying | Regulates Blood Sugars | Soothes Mood |
|---|---|---|---|---|---|---|---|
| • |  |  | • |  | • | • |  |
| • | • |  |  |  | • | • | • |
| • |  | • | • |  | • | • |  |
| • | • | • |  | • | • | • |  |
| • | • | • | • |  | • | • |  |
|  | • |  | • |  | • | • | • |
|  | • | • | • |  | • | • |  |
|  | • |  |  | • | • | • |  |
|  | • |  |  | • | • | • |  |
|  | • |  | • |  | • | • |  |
|  | • |  | • |  | • |  |  |
|  |  |  | • |  |  | • | • |
|  | • |  | • |  |  | • | • |
|  | • | • |  |  |  | • |  |
|  | • |  | • | • | • | • |  |
|  | • |  | • |  |  | • |  |
|  | • |  |  | • | • | • | • |
|  | • |  | • |  | • | • | • |
|  | • |  |  |  |  | • |  |
| • |  |  |  |  |  | • |  |
| • | • |  |  |  | • | • | • |
| • |  |  |  |  | • | • |  |
| • |  |  |  |  | • | • |  |
|  |  |  |  |  |  | • |  |
| • |  | • | • |  |  | • |  |
| • |  | • |  |  |  | • |  |
|  |  |  |  | • |  | • |  |
|  | • |  |  |  |  | • |  |
|  |  |  |  |  |  | • |  |
| • |  |  | • | • |  | • |  |
| • | • | • | • |  | • | • |  |
| • |  |  | • |  |  | • |  |
| • | • | • |  | • | • | • |  |
| • |  |  | • |  |  | • |  |
| • | • |  | • |  | • | • |  |
| • |  | • |  |  | • | • |  |
| • |  |  | • |  | • | • |  |
|  | • |  | • | • |  | • |  |
|  | • | • | • |  |  | • |  |
| • | • | • | • |  | • | • |  |
| • | • | • | • |  | • | • |  |

| Recipes | Cancer Fighting | Heart Healthy | Brain Boosting | Anti-Inflammatory |
|---|---|---|---|---|
| Spiced Parsnip and Sweet Potato Coins, p. 117 | • | • | • | • |
| Za'atar-Roasted Cauliflower, p. 118 | • | • | • | |
| Ruby Red Beet Salad, p. 120 | • | • | • | • |
| Herbs Galore Farro, p. 121 | • | • | • | • |
| Zesty Zucchini Salad, p. 123 | • | • | • | • |
| Warm Fennel Salad, p. 124 | • | • | • | • |
| Spiced-Up Crispy Chickpeas: Vegitude, p. 125 | • | | • | • |
| Spiced-Up Crispy Chickpeas: All-Purpose Savory Blend, p. 125 | • | • | • | • |
| Spiced-Up Crispy Chickpeas: Chili Powder, p. 125 | • | • | • | • |
| Immune Support Yellow Quinoa with Parsley and Almonds, p. 126 | • | • | • | • |
| Turmeric Tahini Dip, p. 129 | • | • | • | • |
| Spicy Vinaigrette, p. 130 | • | • | • | • |
| Green Goddess Fenugreek Tahini Sauce, p. 131 | • | • | • | • |
| Beller Basic Vinaigrette, p. 133 | • | • | • | |
| Chimichurri Sauce, p. 134 | • | • | • | |
| Vegan Caesar Dressing, p. 135 | • | • | • | • |
| Hummus 3 Ways (or More!), p. 138 | • | • | • | |
| Frozen 'Nana "Sandwiches," p. 139 | • | • | • | • |
| Popped Sorghum (or Popcorn) Your Way: Sweet with Heat, p. 141 | • | • | • | • |
| Popped Sorghum (or Popcorn) Your Way: Cheesy and Savory, p. 141 | • | • | • | • |
| Vegan Chocolate Truffles, p. 142 | • | • | • | • |
| Spiced Nut and Date Bars, p. 145 | • | • | • | • |
| Chai-Poached Pears, p. 146 | • | • | • | • |
| Mexican Chili-Lime Fruit Salad, p. 149 | • | • | • | • |
| Chocolate Date "Nice Cream," p. 150 | • | • | • | • |

| Good for the Gut | Helps Digestion | Immune Boosting | Promotes Weight Loss | Bloat Reducing | Detoxifying | Regulates Blood Sugars | Soothes Mood |
|---|---|---|---|---|---|---|---|
|  | • |  | • | • | • | • |  |
| • | • |  | • |  |  |  |  |
|  | • |  | • | • |  | • |  |
|  |  |  |  | • | • | • |  |
|  | • |  |  | • | • | • |  |
|  | • |  |  | • | • | • |  |
| • |  | • |  |  | • | • |  |
| • |  | • | • |  | • | • |  |
| • |  | • | • |  |  | • |  |
|  | • | • | • | • | • | • |  |
|  | • |  | • |  | • | • |  |
| • | • | • | • |  |  | • |  |
|  | • |  | • | • | • | • |  |
|  | • |  | • |  |  |  |  |
| • |  | • |  | • |  | • |  |
|  | • |  | • |  | • | • |  |
|  |  |  | • |  |  |  |  |
|  |  |  |  |  |  | • | • |
|  | • |  |  |  |  | • |  |
| • |  | • |  |  |  | • |  |
|  | • |  | • |  |  | • | • |
|  | • |  |  | • | • | • |  |
|  | • |  | • | • | • | • |  |
| • | • | • | • |  |  | • |  |
|  |  |  |  |  |  | • | • |

# Acknowledgments

I am very excited to have this opportunity to express my gratitude and thank some very special people in my life for their love, ongoing support, and encouragement.

To the following fabulous members of the team at the Beller Nutritional Institute:

Leanna Tu—a huge thank-you! You know how to give heart and soul. You are a true genius, and this book would not have come together without you. You've managed to keep me and this project on track. Your knowledge and expertise through every process of fact-checking, researching, and writing were invaluable. I can't thank you enough for your hard work and sincere dedication to this project.

Freddy Nager, I thank you for your creativity and inspiration, and for always putting a smile on my face no matter how stressful things get. Kimberly Tronic, thank you for being such a rock star and always keeping a creative eye on just about everything. You inspire so many, and I think of you as a warrior.

Tanya Bitcon, thank you for your hard work and to all the research assistants and interns at Beller Nutritional Institute, who are always ready for anything thrown their way, thank you for staying late and always keeping track of details and deadlines.

To my editors, Amanda Englander and Lydia O'Brien: Thank you both for your brilliant ideas and for spearheading the creative process of this book to the finish line. All of your suggestions and modifications kept me going.

To the team at Clarkson Potter, including Ian Dingman, Serena Wang, and Kelli Tokos for making the interior of this book look amazing. Thank you for your tremendous support in allowing me to provide an opportunity to share an easy and delicious means for so many to add daily power through spicing.

And to Andrea Portanova and Natalie Yera for a wonderful marketing and publicity program to get *Power Spicing* out into the world.

To the incomparable Teri-Lynn Fisher, my photographer extraordinaire, who makes even the most complex creative process seem effortless. Thank you for capturing my recipes so beautifully. Thank you, Jenny Park, for being a food-styling genius. You made the food and all the recipes look so incredibly delicious.

A big thank-you to my agent, Dan Strone. After all these years and all of my books, you continue to inspire, enlighten, and enhance my message and my professional career. You are my guiding light on this project.

To my entertainment attorney, Ken Suddleson. Thank you for always having my back, never saying no, and being a tireless advocate for my best interests.

To my patients. Thank you for bringing me into your lives and allowing me to share my passion and knowledge. It is my greatest hope to empower each and every one of you to forever change the way you think about the foods you choose to eat.

To my friends and colleagues—your support and enthusiasm for my passion projects mean the world to me. You are the best at taste-testing my recipes and spice blends, and making sure I'm always within the realm of delicious and nutritious.

A huge thank-you to my family. You guys are my love and support for everything.  To my three big brothers, my sisters and brothers-in-law, nieces, and nephews. I'm so blessed to have such a loving, supportive family. To my mother-in-law, Sheila: You keep me laughing, loving, and always bring a smile to my face.  To my father-in-law, you are deeply missed and I'll love you always.

To my incredible mother and best friend, Shula: Thank you for always believing in me and supporting my dreams, and for always reminding me that life is an adventurous ride and we are never too old to do anything. To my father, Joe: You are the spark plug and single biggest inspiration for my life's work and mission. I carry you with me always, and I miss you so much.

To my amazing kids Alexia, Jonah, Keira, and Evan: Thank you for being who you are and for all your love, humor, honesty, and laughter, and for sometimes taste-testing my creations. Being your mom has made me the luckiest woman in the world.

My soul mate, my husband, Mark. I LOVE YOU! You are an awesome husband and an amazing daddy to our four kids, and you enrich my life and I love always having you by my side. Your enthusiasm and friendship provide me with daily inspiration. Thank you for ALWAYS being there and loving me.

And finally to YOU, the reader! There would be no book without you. Thank you!

# Index

Library of Congress Cataloging-in-Publication Data
Names: Beller, Rachel, author.
Title: Power spicing / Rachel Beller.
Description: First edition. | New York : Clarkson Potter/Publishers, [2019] |
    Includes bibliographical references and index.
Identifiers: LCCN 2018054980 (print) | LCCN 2018056569 (ebook) | ISBN
    9780525574675 (Ebook) | ISBN 9780525574668 (hardcover)
Subjects: LCSH: Cooking (Spices) | Functional foods. | Health. | LCGFT:
    Cookbooks.
Classification: LCC TX819.A1 (ebook) | LCC TX819. A1 B366 2019 (print) | DDC
    641.6/383—dc23
LC record available at https://lccn.loc. gov/2018054980

ISBN 978-0-525-57466-8
Ebook ISBN 978-0-525-57467-5

Printed in China

Book and cover design by Ian Dingman
Cover photographs by Teri Lyn Fisher

10 9 8 7 6 5 4 3 2 1

First Edition